: Mythology of the Lenape :

Mythology of the Lenape

: *Guide and Texts* :

John Bierhorst

THE UNIVERSITY OF ARIZONA PRESS
Tucson

The University of Arizona Press

♾ This book is printed on acid-free, archival-quality paper.
Typography by Jane Byers Bierhorst
Manufactured in the United States of America
00 99 98 97 96 95   6 5 4 3 2 1
Library of Congress Cataloging-in-Publication Data
Bierhorst, John.
Mythology of the Lenape : guide and texts / John Bierhorst.
p. cm.
Includes bibliographical references (p.   ) and index.
ISBN 0-8165-1523-9 (cloth : acid-free paper) — ISBN 0-8165-1573-5 (pbk.: acid-free)
1. Delaware mythology. 2. Delaware mythology—Abstracts. I. Title.
E99.D2B54–1995 398.2′089′973—dc20 95-11567 CIP

British Library Cataloguing-in-Publication Data
A catalogue record for this book is available
from the British Library.

Cover illustration by Tom Fitzpatrick

Turtle Petroglyph, American Indian Rock Carving
Found along the Bronx River on the grounds of the New York Botanical Garden, The Bronx, N.Y., it was probably carved sometime between A.D. 1000 and A.D. 1600. The turtle figures prominently in the Munsee-speaking Delaware Indians' creation myth in which the earth is viewed as an island surrounded by water. The carapace of the tortoise forms the island or "earth-dome" on which humans lived. The turtle may represent a clan symbol of the Indians who occupied the area prior to the coming of Europeans. This petroglyph was found by NYC Landmarks Preservation Commission archaeologists as part of a Design Through Archaeology Program in cooperation with the NYC Department of Cultural Affairs, with support from the National Endowment for the Arts.

Contents

Preface

The purpose of the present work is to give an overview of Lenape, or Delaware, mythology; to place it (tentatively) in its Northeast context; and to make available previously unpublished texts from the collections of M. R. Harrington and Truman Michelson.

The term *mythology,* as used here, embraces all Unami and Munsee Delaware narratives that appear to be formulaic, including myths, folktales, and traditional histories. Generally excluded are personal reminiscences, war exploits, dreams, and visions.

Two hundred eighteen texts are thus accounted for, plus several dubious items included for the sake of completeness. All pre-1965 sources known to exist have been examined, as well as most sources for the period 1965–1992 (excluding a few recent collections not yet available for study).

Grateful acknowledgment is made to the many individuals and institutions who have supplied materials for this work. Their names will be found among the sources asterisked in the bibliography. A special word of thanks is extended to James Rementer, secretary of the Delaware Culture Preservation Committee, Dewey, Oklahoma, for general assistance and for providing unpublished texts; Haig Meshejian, West Shokan, New York, for the use of his personal library; Bruce Pearson, Department of English, University of South Carolina, Columbia, for making available his Delaware field notes; Nancy Rosoff and the National Museum of the American Indian, New York, for facilitating the study of the Harrington collection; the staff of the National Anthropological Archives, Smithsonian Institution, Washington, for giving ready and repeated access to the Michelson, Curtin-Hewitt, and Gilliland collections; the Delaware Resource Center, Trailside Museum, Cross River, New York, for granting access to its tape archive; and the American Philosophical Society, Philadelphia, for copies of manuscript materials in its Delaware collections, especially the Frank G. Speck papers.

A Note on Orthography

Phonological variations within Munsee Delaware and within Unami Delaware are to be observed in transcriptions made at different times and different locations. Delaware terms that appear in the following pages, therefore, are not always consistent, and no attempt has been made to regularize them. The orthography of each source, wherever cited, has been preserved unchanged. Or, where a Delaware term appears in a general discussion, a specific authority is cited for the orthography, using his or her initials in parentheses immediately following the term. Abbreviations for the authorities are as follows:

BP	(Bruce Pearson)
CV	(C. F. Voegelin)
GT	(Gladys Tantaquidgeon)
IG	(Ives Goddard)
JDP	(John Dyneley Prince)
JR	(James Rementer)
MH	(M. R. Harrington)

In general, the various systems for writing Delaware recognize five vowels (*a, e, i, o, u*), each of which may be either long or short. Long vowels have more or less the usual continental values (*ah, eh, ee, oh, oo*); these are indicated by no marking whatever, or by doubling the vowel, or by writing the vowel with an overbar (macron), or by following the vowel with a raised dot, or—especially in older writing—by abandoning the continental analogy and attempting to follow the "rules" of English orthography. Short vowels, likewise, have sometimes been written with no marking; sometimes they appear with a breve. One system (used in Dean's *Lessons*) marks them with a grave accent: *à* (as the *u* in *cup*), *è* (as in *met*), *ì* (as in *fit*), *ò* (as in *north*), and *ù* (as in *pull*). In addition there is an "obscure" vowel, like the *a* in the English word *sofa,* often indicated by the upside-down *e,* or schwa; for this vowel Dean's system uses the symbol *ë*. Consonants are as in English, except that *x* has a throaty sound like the German *ch* in *ach;* and *th* is always two separate sounds, as in the English word *hothead.* Delaware words are ordinarily stressed on the next-to-last syllable, but there are many exceptions.

The foregoing description by no means exhausts the subtleties of Delaware phonology and its orthographic representations. For further explanation of phonetic symbols see Pullum and Ladusaw, *Phonetic Symbol Guide;* Sturtevant, *Handbook,* vol. 15, pp. x–xi. For Delaware (i.e., Lenape) applications, see Dean, *Lessons;* Goddard, *Morphology;* Pearson, *Grammar;* and Voegelin, "Delaware."

: Mythology of the Lenape :

Introduction

Historically the Lenape are among the best-known peoples of North America, both in the native and nonnative worlds. As recently as the eighteenth century their primacy was recognized by fellow Algonquians of the eastern seaboard, who referred to them as "our grandfathers." During the same century the Iroquois found it necessary to label them "women" in order to reduce their influence.[1] Among nonnatives the Lenape, or Delaware, are celebrated as the original owners of what is now the continent's most populous metropolitan region: these are the people said to have sold Manhattan Island to the Dutch for somewhat less than its value (a topic enshrined not only in Euro-American but also in Lenape folklore),[2] who subsequently gained prominence for their role in colonial treaty conferences and in the American Revolution.[3] Thomas Jefferson himself, whose far-ranging interests extended to ethnography, published a Lenape legend.[4]

It would follow that Lenape oral literature should be well known. That it is not can be charged to accident and missed opportunities. Although there have been substantive collections of Lenape narrative lore, these have been small; or, if larger, they have been published poorly, partially, or not at all.

Amounting to a not inconsiderable total of 218 texts—as recognized by the present study—this literature has value for its long glimpse into the spiritual and aesthetic life of a classic American people. Owing to the flexibility of bilingual narrators, it offers a linguistic resource for students of the two surviving Lenape languages, Unami and Munsee, as well as a purely literary corpus in colorful, full-bodied English. It is also rich in ethnographic detail. And, not least, it provides grist for the folklorist who may wish to address such questions as, What is the geographical context of Lenape lore? How, if at all, has it changed over the centuries? The second of these questions will provide a convenient starting point.

The Lenape Exodus

When Dutch and Swedish settlers arrived in the seventeenth century, the Lenape held a territory that extended along the Atlantic Coast from the mouth of the Delaware River to the western end of Long Island Sound and up the Hudson three-quarters of the way to the site of present Albany. Since the easternmost groups were pushed westward almost immediately, it has not been easy to determine the original ethnic boundary, especially east of the Hudson; and the question has led to disagreement among historians.

In the 1970s, however, the linguist Ives Goddard, using scraps of evidence scattered in old documents, was able to propose a definition of the Lenape homeland that has gained wide acceptance.[5] Following Goddard's lead, the boundaries of the territory occupied by those who spoke Munsee dialects may now be drawn to include the five boroughs of New York City and the southwest corner of Nassau County, Long Island (with the rest of Long Island assigned to non-Lenape Algonquians). Northward the boundary follows the Connecticut-New York line to the southwest corner of Massachusetts; from there due west to the northeast corner of Pennsylvania; then south-southwest to the vicinity of present-day Scranton; from Scranton, to the Delaware Water Gap and across the present state of New Jersey to the Atlantic Ocean immediately southeast of Staten Island.

The remainder of New Jersey southward, the Philadelphia metropolitan area, and the state of Delaware (except its southwestern third) comprise the region in which the so-called Unami dialects were spoken. Unami and Munsee, each taken as a whole, are regarded as separate languages, though very closely related. Among the Unami, native speakers call themselves *lənά·p·e* (IG)—the Munsee variant is *lə̀nά·pe·w* (IG)—meaning "ordinary person" or "real person." The redundant form *ləni-lənά·p·e,* or "real Lenape," written in English as Lenni-Lenape, was once commonly heard but has now fallen into disuse. Still another term, Unalachtigo, encountered in older ethnographies, refers to a division of the Unami that has long since ceased to exist as an identifiable group. The tribal name Delaware, taken from the Delaware River, first appeared in the seventeenth century and has continued to be widely used by outsiders and by the Lenape themselves.

During the eighteenth century both the Munsee and the Unami, often in close association, left the ancestral homeland for points west. During the Revolution the main body were in east central Ohio. Following the treaty of 1795, most moved to the White River area of east central Indiana. By that time others had taken up residence in southern Ontario and a small group of Munsees had found their way to the Cattaraugus Seneca Reservation south of Buffalo.

Driven from Indiana, Delawares were in Kansas at the outbreak of the

Civil War. After the war, again forced to give up their settlements, Kansas Delawares moved to the Bartlesville area of what is now eastern Oklahoma. Meanwhile, another smaller group had migrated by way of Texas to the vicinity of Anadarko, fifty miles southwest of present Oklahoma City. Thus the migration, finally, came to a close.[6]

The preceding list of places gives only the outline of the Lenape exodus. But it mentions every geographical area from which Lenape folklore has been recorded. The principal Lenape communities today are in Oklahoma (at Bartlesville in Washington County and at Anadarko in Caddo County) and in Ontario at Six Nations, Moraviantown, and Muncy Town. At present, Unami is spoken by a few older people in Oklahoma; Munsee, by a few in Ontario.

First recorded in the 1650s, folk traditions are still remembered, even if distantly, in the early 1990s—at least in Oklahoma. Evidently twentieth-century Lenape lore retains links with the native past, yet the extent of this continuity can be seen only in part.

One problem is that the very earliest chroniclers recorded no more than a few fragments of Lenape mythology. Another difficulty is that the sober-minded earlier writers were interested in history and religion rather than in literature, or folklore, per se. Therefore, child-hero tales, campfire yarns, and animal stories that might have been heard two or three hundred years ago went unreported. By and large the more secular narratives are confined to twentieth-century collections, yet this in itself does not mean that they are new.

Two themes with long continuity are the turtle whose back forms either the earth or its substitute and the culture hero who departs, promising to return in the future. These show up during the earliest period, 1655–1680 (texts 1 and 2),[7] again between 1805 and 1824 (texts 9 and 11), yet again between 1883 and 1905 (texts 44 and 49), and once more in the mid-twentieth century (texts 127 and 187).

A theme well known since at least the eighteenth century (text 17) is the legendary trickery of the early Dutch settlers, still being rehashed in the late 1900s (text 219). Yet another is the origin of the Pleiades, known in modern versions (texts 157, 171) and traceable to at least 1822 (text 26).

Among apparent losses are the culture hero regarded as a hare (not recorded after 1883), the emergence of ancestors from beneath the earth (1824), and the exploits of twin demiurges (preserved as the faintest of echoes in text 152, recorded in 1969).

Iroquois, especially Seneca, influence can be sensed in several of the stories told by latter-day Lenape. Ball Player (text 71), a version of the widespread type The Bride and the Brothers, from a Unami teller, might well have been adapted from a Seneca source—the name of the monster, yahquaha, is from the Seneca language. Seneca terms also crop up in the tales told by Munsee speaker John Armstrong (texts 41–46). But at least two of these stories (41, 43) have no counterparts in Seneca tradition, three include Lenape terms (41, 42, 44), and all, with the possible exception of text 46, contain personages such as the Lenapean twelve women (41), the Munsee demiurge Moskim (44), and the fish spirits pike and sunfish (42, 44, 45), not to be found in Seneca lore.

Nonnative intrusions may also be detected, but they are minimal. Although by the twentieth century a few Bible stories had worked their way into the repertory, they are poorly developed, even perfunctory. There is no Life of Christ and no story of Adam and Eve. As for European folktales, there are strong hints of three or four well-known types, including Jack the Numskull, but the evidence is not conclusive.

In general, Lenape lore has retained its Indianness. Moreover, despite the far displacement of the people themselves, their traditional narratives, folkloristically speaking, still belong to the old homeland in the Northeast.

The Narratives as a Whole

The geographical origin of a particular body of folklore, ideally, can be determined by a close look at its constituent parts. Since folklore grows by borrowing, the themes, principal characters, and tale types of one people's oral traditions usually owe much to those of their regional neighbors, and vice versa.

In North America, mythological provinces, so to speak, may be recognized for the Southwest, the Plains, the Northwest Coast, and other regions. In the Northeast, a province of more or less cohesive traditions would include Seneca, Cayuga, Onondaga, Oneida, Mohawk, Susquehanna, Huron (or Wyandot), Shawnee, Lenape, Mahican, Nanticoke, Montagnais-Naskapi, and the various Algonquian groups of New England, eastern Long Island, and southeastern Canada.[8]

Unfortunately the folklore of those tribes that lived adjacent to the Lenape homeland—Nanticoke, Susquehanna, Mahican, and the southeastern New England Algonquians—is largely unrecorded. But because oral traditions have a longer reach than the immediate neighborhood, there is still sufficient material upon which to base a few conclusions.

It may be argued that the most important tale type in any tradition is the one that attracts to itself the endless string of episodes accounting for the origin of the world and the institution of human customs. In North America one of the most prominent stories of this class is the so-called Woman Who Fell from the Sky, a tale belonging to the Northeast (though it has been borrowed by the easternmost of the midwestern Ojibwa groups). The myth relates the trials of a woman ejected from her home in the sky, who lands on earth and gives birth to twin sons; in a series of standard adventures the family establishes the physical and social world, preparing the earth for human habitation. This epic has been reported for most of the Iroquois nations (Cayuga, Mohawk, Onondaga, Seneca), the Iroquoian Huron and Wyandot, and the Algonquian Shawnee—as well as the Lenape.

Another important tale, too fluid to be called a type, is the saga of the ambiguous hero who embodies the soul of the people, even if his adventures are almost always mishaps. For the New England Algonquians this character is represented by various animal tricksters and, in part, by the major hero Gluskap. For the Iroquoians, the character is the mischievous twin son of the woman who fell from the sky. Probably Lenape lore formerly made more of this mischievous, or evil, son than it has in recent generations.

In any case the Lenape figure who most clearly corresponds to the stereotypical trickster is not the son of the sky woman but the folk hero known to the Unami as Wehixamukes. Significantly, the stock situation—which casts Wehixamukes as a man who misunderstands—aligns with a tale type that belongs to the Northeast region and has been reported, specifically, for the Cayuga, Onondaga, Seneca, Wyandot, and Micmac (one of the Algonquian tribes of southeastern Canada).

It should be mentioned that although the various Northeast Indian tales about the "man who misunderstands" seem to echo European yarns of the figure referred to by folklorists as "the literal fool" and "Jack the Numskull," the Native American details are decidedly different, implying that the similarity may be no more than a coincidence. In Native American tradition the theme is usually of slight importance, giving rise to isolated stories. Only among the Lenape does it form an extended cycle.

Aside from the creation epic and the trickster cycle, the body of Lenape narratives exhibits numerous points of contact with Northeast tradition. Although a statistical summary of tale types will not demonstrate a precise fit, it serves to indicate the relationship in broad outline. The seven tribal traditions that have the greatest overlap (four tale types or more) with the Lenape, along with the number of types each shares with Lenape, are as follows: Seneca (15), Onondaga (8), Shawnee (8), Wyandot (6), Ojibwa

(5), Menominee (5), and Cherokee (4). Of these seven, the last three belong to the Midwest (Ojibwa, Menominee) and the Southeast (Cherokee). Among the tales types in question are Bear Boy, Bride and the Brothers, Hunters and the Water Monster, Serpent's Bride, and Turtle Who Carried the People. These and others may be traced in Part Four of the Guide, Comparative Notes.

Such an examination does not prove that the Lenape had all of these shared stories when they lived in New York and New Jersey three hundred years ago. But in folkloristic terms it does suggest that the Lenape, whether through retention or latter-day borrowing, have maintained their identity as a Northeast people.

The Principal Characters

Lenape narratives are devoted to a variety of major and minor characters more or less human or at least susceptible to personification. Most if not all of them may be classed by the Unami term *manëtuwàk* (JR), "spirits" (singular, *manëtu*). It is instructive to examine the stories closely, to see how these personages relate to one another and how they may have changed over the centuries.

Of special prominence is the so-called Great Spirit, regarded as the supreme being and evidently synonymous with the Creator, Our Creator, Master of Life, God, Great God, and Good Spirit. Recorded Unami terms are *ki·š·e·ləmúk·ɔnkw* (IG), "our creator"; *ketanëtuwit* (JR), "greatest of all spirits"; and *welsit manə́tu*, "good spirit" (JR).[9] A Munsee term imperfectly recorded in northern New Jersey in 1679–80 as *kickeron*, or *kickerom*, may be written in modern Munsee as *kihkayə́mna* (IG), "our chief."[10]

The stories relate that the Creator made all things (text 27); specifically, he shaped the earth out of mud (187),[11] created humans (25), and made useful plants (152). In one myth the Creator plays the role of transformer, reducing the man-eating squirrel to its present, harmless proportions (162). Likewise, it was the Great Spirit who decreed the extinction of the dangerous prehistoric mastodon (47).

The Great Spirit, or God, is also seen as a teacher, who gave "churches" to all nations (96). Picturesquely, it is told that he came down one winter wearing snowshoes and taught the Delawares their customs and ceremonies (20). He taught the rites of the Delaware "church," or Big House (89), and in time gave Delawares the new Peyote Religion (109). Munsees have said that the carved face in the oldtime Big House represented the Creator himself (119).

The supreme being repays ceremonial lapses with anger, sending a disastrous snowfall (28) or an earthquake (104, 157). But "the great father Jesus" can also be merciful, revealing a miraculous source of corn during a winter famine (138).

It is told that when his work on earth was finished, the Great Spirit retired (25), telling the people to depute a chief in his place (24). Today he resides in the sky and may be visited there by humans fortunate or gifted enough to make the journey (6).

Both in this world and in the next the Great Spirit's work is challenged by the Evil Spirit, or Devil, called Mahtantu (JR) by the Unami, Muttóntoe (JDP) by the Munsee. It is told that the Devil, or Mahtantu, against the wishes of the Creator, made bats (27) and poisonous plants (152). Muttóntoe, it is said, is the death spirit, who comes to steal the living (66); and in one story the Devil is described as punishing the wicked in the afterworld (36). It was the Devil, moreover, who taught Europeans the arts of civilization (85).

Over the generations, stories about the Great Spirit have evidently multiplied, while stories of the demiurge Hare have dwindled and disappeared. Called Tschimammus (hare) in a now-extinct dialect of Unami,[12] or Moskim in old Munsee lore,[13] Hare is the elder of the twin sons born to the woman who fell from the sky. According to an old account, Tschimammus was "one of the twins born to the woman that was thrown from heaven"; he was the "great God" who made the land, then retired from the earth, promising one day to return; he now dwells in the sky world, where humans may visit him (11).

Of Moskim it is said that he was born first, followed by his twin brother, who killed their mother by exiting through her navel (44). Such lore is more fully developed in extant Iroquois versions, where the various contests between the good twin and the evil twin are related at length. In modern Lenape tradition, the twin story has survived only as an abbreviated account of the Creator's trials with his adversary, Mahtantu (152).

Similar in some respects to Moskim, or Tschimammus, is the trickster-hero Wehixamukes, known in English as Jack, Crazy Jack, the "strong man," or the "Delaware Sampson." The Unami term *wēhīxamūkēs* (BP) does not seem to be translatable, though the late Frank Speck offered the folk etymology "one who mixes," perhaps inspired by the tale in which the trickster misapplies the instruction to mix meal at the water hole and, instead, mixes meal *in* the water hole.[14] But foolishness is only one aspect of the trickster's personality.

Like the hero-god Hare, Wehixamukes was a "great" man (23) who worked "miracles" (127); he engaged in a series of contests with a companion-adversary, variously described as his partner (97) or his nephew (50); eventually he departed from the earth, promising to return (97, 127).

Armed with these observations, we may look back speculatively to the first Lenape story on record, the tale of the "miracle" worker sketchily paraphrased by the Swedish engineer Peter Lindeström in his journal of 1654–56. According to Lindeström, the hero ascended to the sky, promising to return; later, another "teacher," bearded and with a large mouth (like Europeans), came among the people, and he, too, disappeared, promising to return (1).

Probably the second hero is Christ. His predecessor, conceivably, is Wehixamukes, or, more plausibly, Tschimammus-Moskim.

The Lesser Characters

Of secondary importance in narrative lore—though paramount in ritual—is the Mask Being, known to the Unami as *Mĭsinghâli'kŭn* (MH), or simply Misingw, or Mesingw (mask). In the Big House ceremony, the principal Lenape rite (formerly held each fall for a period of twelve days), the role of the Mask Being was played by an impersonator who wore a bearskin robe and a mask half black, half red. Faces carved in the houseposts of the Big House itself were said to represent this supernatural (96, 114).

Naturally, the Mask Being is mentioned in the various myths of the origin of the Big House, where it is often stated that he instituted the rite, instructing the first participants (48, 88, 96). Alive in the sky world, the Mask Being and his brethren, or the company of mask beings, are overseers of human morality (126). Evidently *Mĭsinghâli'kŭn* is also the Lenape animal master, the spirit who controls the availability of game, especially deer (88)—though oldtime Lenape sometimes assigned this role to the mysterious "white deer."[15]

Yet another game master is the diminutive man, or boy, known to the Unami as Wemategunis (MH), or *Maté·kanis* (GT). It has been said that *Maté·kanis* rides the back of a deer and herds game, hiding it from hunters (133). In one story the little man is a trickster with a penchant for mimicry, thus earning the name "Answer-me," or echo (70). More often, however, he is kind and helpful, appearing unexpectedly to aid a distressed hero or heroine (66, 132, 202).

Other personages that may be both helpful and unhelpful include Mother Corn, Snow Boy, the Sun, and the Thunders. These are supernaturals who are either unpredictable or whose favors are contingent upon human cooperation.

In the case of Mother Corn, people lose her completely if they fail to pay her proper respect. In her absence crops fail and starvation sets in. But she reappears if it is determined that the people have suffered long enough (29), especially if they fulfill certain ceremonial obligations (67, 117).

By contrast, Snow Boy's very presence signals danger, particularly for children, who run the risk of losing their extremities to frostbite. If kept at a distance, however, and if appeased through ceremonial offerings, the spirit benefits travelers by offering an ice bridge for crossing streams (211); and he helps hunters by providing the snow cover that enables them to track game (72, 108).

The Sun, called "our uncle" (215) or "elder brother,"[16] is generally beneficent and seldom feared.[17] In one of the best-known Unami stories, he aids a pair of boy heroes by giving them hot ashes to kill a water monster (84, 99). In one version, however, the Sun refuses, and the boys have to go for help to the Moon (125). At night, it is said, the Sun travels across the earth in the form of a man. At this time, according to a Munsee story, he is evidently at his most dangerous, entering people's homes in search of human blood (76).

Also unpredictable are the Thunders, called *pléthoak* (42) or *pălé·săwak* (IG) by the Munsee, *pe·thakhuwé·yɔk* (IG) by the Unami. These powerful creatures are manlike but at the same time are thought of as birds: "partridge" (probably ruffed grouse),[18] eagle,[19] and turkey[20] are the species variously mentioned. In one story the Thunders are said to have prevented a man from marrying (53); in another, they strike an innocent woman dead (163); in still other tales they are ominously reported as dining on "bone soup" (164, 195).

On the other hand, Thunders can be counted on to do battle against their proverbial enemy, the horned serpent, rescuing humans in the process (86, 142).

The horned serpent, or great horned snake, known to the Unami as *mëxaxkuk* (JR), to the Munsee as *w'aXkōk,*[21] is one of the consistently menacing supernaturals in Lenape lore. Often called simply "the water monster," this creature lives in a rock den within a river and displays an unwholesome interest in sex. Either the monster gives a young man the power to attract women irresistibly (57) or it itself takes the form of a man, impregnating young women (86, 202). In one story the people are forced to sacrifice a young woman to the serpent in order to avert a plague (143);

in another, young heroes kill the monster and preserve its scales as a rain charm (64).

A similar beast, sometimes confused with *mëxaxkuk,* is the swallowing monster, called *wewtənúwe·s* (CV), roughly translated into English as "mermaid" (even though the animal is often male). It may also be called "fish," but it is fishlike only from the waist down; the head and upper body are human.[22] Generally a man-eater pure and simple (125, 160, 170), *wewtənúwe·s,* like *mëxaxkuk,* has an unwelcome interest in sex. Male "mermaids" are said to seduce or impregnate young women (160, 200); in one story a female "mermaid" detains a young man as a prisoner of love (82). Possibly the mysterious young woman with blue and green hair, who indirectly causes the deaths of a whole family of brothers (71), is a cryptic "mermaid."

Another of the unpersuadable supernaturals is the outsized *ya'kwahe* (MH), known in English as great bear or naked bear. The strange Lenape term is evidently an adaptation of the Seneca *nyáʔkwaehe:h,*[23] well known in Iroquois lore as the name for a hairless bearlike monster, all but impossible to extirpate.[24] In one of the Lenape stories the *ya'kwahe,* after consuming human victims, is magically killed with the aid of animal helpers (71). In another tale the creature is identified with the prehistoric mastodon, annihilated by decree of the Great Spirit himself (47).

Finally, there is the horrific *mhú·we* (CV), or cannibal giant, who sweeps down from the north country, sometimes in considerable numbers. *Mhú·we* (126), also called *mamuui* (204) or, by the Munsee, *má·le·w*[25] bears an obvious relationship to the ice-hearted cannibal, *chenoo,*[26] of the New England and eastern Canadian Algonquians; the cannibal ice-giant, *windigo,*[27] of the Ojibwa; and the stone coat, *genonsgwa,*[28] of the Iroquois.

As in giant lore the world over, Lenape giants are stupid (144), even if dangerous. Like other Northeast winter cannibals, the Lenape variety may originate as an ordinary human, transformed by starvation and bitter cold (204). Or, as in the Iroquois case, a human can become a cannibal by rolling in tar and gravel, thus acquiring the typical "stone coat" (204). Indeed, the *mhú·we,* however stupid, appears to be invulnerable—yet it may be killed by a stake driven into its anus (126).

The Storytelling Event

The earliest description of Lenape storytelling appears in the journal of the Dutch traveler Jasper Danckaerts for the year 1679. According to this often-reprinted passage, an eighty-year-old native man of Hackensack,

New Jersey, (evidently a Munsee), in reply to the traveler's query about the origin of his people,

> was silent for a little while . . . then took a piece of coal out of the fire where he sat, and began to write upon the floor. He first drew a circle, a little oval, to which he made four paws or feet, a head and a tail. "This," said he, "is a tortoise, lying in the water around it," and he moved his hand round the figure, continuing, "This was or is all water, and so at first was the world or the earth, when the tortoise gradually raised its round back up high, and the water ran off of it, and thus the earth became dry." He then took a little straw and placed it on end in the middle of the figure, and proceeded, "The earth was now dry, and there grew a tree. . . ."[29]

An account such as this offers some slight evidence that stories were at one time preserved in pictographs or at least that improvised pictures might have been used in native recitals. Some 250 years later, in 1933, the knowledgeable Munsee traditionalist Joseph Montour assured Frank Speck that it had formerly been the custom to preserve history—*xo´wek‘hí·kkan* (ancient history)[30]—by means of pictures on wood, called *maxkwala´man* (painted red); but more detailed data were not forthcoming. Speck had elicited the information in order to learn whether there was a native tradition to corroborate the claim of Constantine Rafinesque that the so-called Walam Olum, or Red Score, had been transcribed from pictographs on wooden sticks.[31]

Rafinesque's Walam Olum, a purported Lenape origin legend extant only in Rafinesque's manuscript version (pictures with Lenape glosses), was accepted as genuine by some, though not all, scholars up through the mid-twentieth century, including Speck, M. R. Harrington, and C. F. Voegelin. Confidence in the document has lately faded.[32]

It may be stated with some assurance that the literature of the Lenape represents an oral, rather than a written, tradition. Mnemonic devices, however, may once have been common. Harrington, evidently drawing upon his own ethnographic researches, indicated as much in his fictionalized account of ancient Delaware life entitled *Dickon Among the Lenapes.*[33] And a more reliable statement to the same effect was recorded in 1977 by the late Unami traditionalist Nora Thompson Dean. According to Dean:

> Long, long time ago there were professional storytellers. That's what they did, that was their business. I was told this because that was too

> early in my day. And the storyteller carried a bag, and when he'd tell a story, then he'd remove some of these little rocks, or beads, or seeds, cornseeds, and he'd set those to one side. And after he took care of all these grains, he was exhausted then, the stories was all over. So he'd return 'em to the bag and go to another house, maybe. And they usually gave him a nice meal, Indian meal . . . you could give him tobacco.[34]

The storytelling event itself has been described, briefly, in a manuscript of 1823–24 by the pioneer ethnographer C. C. Trowbridge:

> They will entertain each other a whole night with the ingenious story of a wolf, a raccoon, or of some great hunter [i.e., Wehixamukes?], whose deeds have been handed down by their traditions.[35]

An anonymous report from the same period describes another aspect of the tradition:

> They are great story tellers but will not suffer them to be told except in the winter when the ground is froze lest by so doing they should incur the displeasure of snakes and lizards and they should crawl into bed to them.[36]

Essentially the same admonition is reported by Nora Dean, who adds this recollection concerning stories she heard from her mother (who in turn had heard them from her own mother):

> [Stories were told] just whenever there was a lull in our work, like maybe a rainy day, or something like that . . . then [my mother] would tell us stories. Sometime in the evening she'd tell us stories. Sometime at the dinner table. . . . We was supposed to listen very intently, you know. Of course, in my day it wasn't permitted to ask questions why was this, why was that. You just had to absorb what was told to you.[37]

The female provenance of the stories heard by Nora Dean is in contrast to the long line of male narrators indicated in earlier reports—and, in fact, to the generally male cast of Lenape mythology as implied by the overview of folkloric characters offered above. Dean's repertoire fits well with the materials obtained from men storytellers, but it may be asked whether there were separate strands of tradition for males and females.

In a folktale recorded in 1983 or 1984 by the Anadarko woman Bessie Snake, the guardian of heaven is not the Great Spirit (always referred to in English as "he") but an old woman called "grandmother." Stories of this mother of ghosts, who superintends the affairs of the afterworld, are also known from the Iroquois—presumably from male narrators. But in Lenape lore the idea is not otherwise on record (text 200).

Nora Dean herself, who usually told the origin of the Pleiades as a transformation of seven boys, as would be normal, told it on one occasion as a story about seven girls (text 157). In a tale from the late Martha Ellis, another of the Anadarko traditionalists, the Thunders—otherwise always male—are replaced by a troupe of twelve women, who, like typical Thunders, kill and eat the horned serpent (text 202).

In 1977, discovering that Martha Ellis had heard off-color tales from her brother and that there had been Lenape "men's stories," the linguist Ralph Cooley attempted to elicit the texts. Ellis resisted. Cooley, tape recorder in hand, pressed Ellis to let down her guard, offering to excuse all men from the room (except himself). She remained politely silent. Then, sensing that she feared embarrassment if Bartlesville Delawares were to hear the tapes, he vowed never to play them in Bartlesville. At last Ellis declared definitively, "I will *not* tell those nasty stories."[38]

Whether there are any exclusively "men's stories" on record would be hard to say. None in the inventory appears to belong in this category, though it may be noted that Nora Dean began her telling of text 168 with the disclaimer that the story might not be suitable for "children's ears."

From Performance to Literature

The act of storytelling makes its way to the printed page in a variety of ways, usually—but not always—eliminating the extraliterary aspects. Among the most striking features of live Delaware performance are the songs that occasionally punctuate fictional or legendary narratives; a few of these have been recorded and are noted in the abstracts for texts 83, 95, 105, 189, and 190. Rarely, audience reaction is recorded, as in text 73, which includes the passage, "Meantime the Turtle just walked across underwater and got the food! (laughter)—but the wolf could do nothing but run up and down the bank and howl."

Although the narrator's gestures are generally lost, vocal emphasis is preserved in tape recordings, which give a heightened sense of personality, even wit. Note this passage from Nora Dean's English-language telling of Bear Boy (text 174): "And finally he became so attached to this bear mother, he thought he was a bear." Rewritten to reveal vocal emphasis, the passage reads, "And finally be became so *attached* to this bear mother, he *thought* he was a bear." Thus the reader comes a little closer to hearing the storyteller's voice.

More substantial than vocal inflection are the rough, flavorful colloquialisms of Delaware English, in which native texts have been re-created, not merely translated, since at least the turn of the twentieth century. Faithfully transcribed, without need for explanation, the prose on the printed page implies the act of storytelling: "He was dirty, lay down anywhere, and had no get up to him," "By crabs!" "The little fish made lots of flops," "They got plumb weak."

The available material does not permit a discussion of Delaware English over the centuries. But the texts preserved from bilingual Unami speakers in eastern Oklahoma between 1907 and 1990 would permit a detailed examination of at least one Delaware milieu. Among the features that might be noted:

1. use of the present-as-past ("those boys went to the hill and turn to stone," "and they went on that evening and camp");
2. selective avoidance of the subjunctive-tainted "were" in favor of the more muscular "was" ("there was two boys very poor and needy," "I wanted to see how strong you was");
3. colloquial use of "right," "sure," and "directly" ("he was right small," "and sure there will be a bear," "directly they heard Wehixamukes hollering");
4. strong adjectives used adverbially ("he reached the bank safe," "they live good and have plenty").

The preceding examples are drawn from the texts reproduced in full in this volume, collected in eastern Oklahoma between 1907 and 1912. (Such examples establish a benchmark against which later English texts from eastern Oklahoma could be profitably compared.) The collectors of these particular texts were M. R. Harrington and Truman Michelson, the first ethnographers to record Delaware English.

The generation that preceded Harrington and Michelson concentrated on getting Lenape stories into the standard, front-parlor English that could be sent to the printer. Thus we have Richard C. Adams's Unami *Legends*, brought out in 1905, and Jeremiah Curtin's Munsee stories from Cattaraugus, collected in the 1880s and finally published in 1923 in his posthumous *Seneca Indian Myths*.[39]

Harrington and Michelson evidently assumed that the stories they had collected (mostly not backed up by native-language versions) were unpublishable. Harrington repeatedly promised a work to be entitled "Lenape Mythology," or "Lenape Folklore," but it did not appear.[40] Years later, in 1938, he brought out several of the tales, reshaped into formal English, in his fictionalized *Dickon Among the Lenapes.* Michelson never published his Lenape narratives at all.

In the 1930s a younger generation of field workers, including Voegelin and Speck, made careful collections of native-language texts, accompanied by lexical glosses and, often, formal English translations. Nearly twenty years later, in 1951–52, a useful inquiry into the folklore of the Oklahoma Delaware was conducted by William W. Newcomb, who published short English versions of traditional narratives, harking back to the pre-Curtin era of sometimes severely abbreviated paraphrases.

In the 1960s, well-prepared linguists began a new wave of collecting that yielded noteworthy results, especially in Oklahoma. Of particular value were the texts recorded at Anadarko by the late Ralph Cooley and at Bartlesville by a group of linguists that included Bruce Pearson and James Rementer. This most recent era was dominated by the forceful presence of Nora Thompson Dean (a native of Dewey, five miles north of Bartlesville), who, until her death in 1984, contributed a steady flow of high-quality texts in both English and Unami. Dean's English-language tellings were recorded especially by Nicholas Shoumatoff, founder of the Delaware Resource Center in Cross River, New York, during 1976 and 1977.

Looking back over the entire record, spanning the 337 years from 1655 to 1992, a vibrant, persistent tradition emerges, obscured in part by faulty transmission and long silences, yet rich in textual detail and eminently worthy of future study.

{ : GUIDE : }

The four-part guide that follows may be viewed as an extended introduction to the selected Harrington and Michelson texts, providing a detailed treatment of the whole corpus of which they form a part. Given in full in the second half of this volume, each of the texts in question is synopsized here, in Part Two of the Guide, where it may be located by the asterisk preceding its assigned number.

The Guide is principally contained in Part Two (Story Abstracts), which provides a synopsis not only of the Harrington and Michelson items but of each of the 218 Lenape stories on record. So that the scope of Lenape mythology can be seen at a glancce, the abstracts are preceded by a thematic outline (Part One). Keyed by abstract number, the outline serves as an analytic table of contents.

Part Three (Stories of Uncertain Origin) may be regarded as an appendix to the abstracts, treating texts that have been rejected.

In Part Four (Comparative Notes) the Lenape narratives are connected to cognate stories from other cultures to show how the Lenape tradition fits in with the mythology of eastern North America as a whole.

PART ONE : Thematic Outline

Numerals preceding the story names refer to abstracts in Part Two, where each abstract takes its place in chronological order, A.D. 1655 to 1992. Thus the numerals give an approximate idea of the age of each telling, or version, with the lowest numbers referring to early sources like Lindeström or Danckaerts and the highest to recordings made as recently as the 1990s.

The outline also shows whether a particular version is Unami or Munsee (so far as can be determined) and whether it has variants outside Delaware tradition. The following abbreviations and symbols are used:

M Munsee Delaware stories from Bayonne, Cattaraugus, New York City area, Ohio (Capt. Pipe), Ontario, or Kansas (Michelson papers)

U Unami Delaware stories from Indiana, Kansas (Morgan's *Journals*), New Sweden, Oklahoma, or Texas.

? Delaware stories, either M or U

Note: Items here labeled "Euro-American," "Pontiac," or "Seneca" have been accepted as at least marginally Delaware despite the non-Delaware provenance.

Underlined name indicates Delaware tale type.

CAPITALIZED name indicates tale type or motif found also outside Delaware tradition.

(Names neither underlined nor capitalized indicate stories obtained from one narrator only, even if more than one telling is on record.)

Creation Epic

2(M). TURTLE ISLAND; HUMANS CREATED FROM TREE

9(U?). DELUGE; EARTH DIVER

10(U?). WOMAN WHO FELL FROM THE SKY; TWIN SONS

11(U?). WOMAN WHO FELL FROM THE SKY; TWIN SONS; HARE AS DEMIURGE

14(U?). WOMAN WHO FELL FROM THE SKY; TWIN SONS

15(?). WOMAN WHO FELL FROM THE SKY; TWIN SONS

30(?). WOMAN WHO FELL FROM THE SKY; EARTH DIVER; TURTLE ISLAND

44–45(M). WOMAN WHO FELL FROM THE SKY; TURTLE ISLAND; TWIN SONS; HARE AS DEMIURGE
46(Seneca). WOMAN WHO FELL FROM THE SKY; TURTLE ISLAND; TWIN SONS; DYING BROTHER
65(U). DELUGE; EARTH DIVER; TURTLE ISLAND
77(U?). EARTH DIVER; TURTLE ISLAND
78(U). TURTLE ISLAND motif
152(U). GOOD AND EVIL CREATORS
187(M). Turtle as EARTH DIVER

Creation Tales

19(?). GOLDEN AGE
32(U?). Origin of humans from thunder
34(U), 39(U?). Origin of Winter with motif MARRIAGE OF THE NORTH AND THE SOUTH
36(U). Origin of mosquitoes. Cf. 7(U) Origin of gnats, 152(U) GOOD AND EVIL CREATORS (evil creator makes insects)
61(U). Origin of love medicine. Cf. 191(U).
124(M). ORIGIN OF AUTUMN HAZE
69(U?). Origin of stories
154(U). Owl's earring becomes bittersweet vine

Transformer Tale

162(U), 181(U?). Creator reduces man-eating squirrel

Emergence

18(M), 21(M?). ANCESTORS EMERGE FROM UNDERWORLD

Legendary Migration

16(U?). MIGRATION FROM THE WEST
81(U?), 198(U). MIGRATION ACROSS OCEAN. Note that 81(U?) includes MIGRATION IN EXPANDING BOAT motif.

Culture Hero/Trickster

1(U). Miracle worker
20(M?). Wise teacher visits earth
23(?), 49–50(U), 79(?), 97(U), 106(M), 107(M), 127(U), 149–150(U), 155–156(U), 167(U), 169(U). Wehixamukes, also called Jack or Crazy Jack (MAN WHO MISUNDERSTANDS). Note that 106(M) represents the type LITERAL FOOL KILLS SLEEPING BABY.
24(M?). Great Spirit was first chief
25(M). CREATION BY THOUGHT; Instructor
51(U), 192(U). FORTUNATE HUNTER

Dangerous Supernaturals

8(U?), 47(U?). Mammoth Legend
41(M). Netyogwesûk (with motifs JONAH and Twelve women)
52(U?). Great Bear
66(M). Youth and his uncle
56(U). Monster brains
72(U), 108(U), 211(U?). Snow Boy
82(U?). Boy and mermaid
75(U). Cyclone
76(M). Sun and cornbread
78(U), 141(U), 191(U). THE HUNTERS AND THE WATER MONSTER. Cf. 163(U). Note that 78(U) has FISHED-UP TURTLE motif.
84(U?), 99(U), 125(U), 160(U), 170(U), 182(U), 195(U). The Water Monster and the Sun. Cf. 64(U?).
93(U). THE TURTLE WHO CARRIED THE PEOPLE, with FISHED-UP TURTLE motif
126(U), 144(U). WINTER CANNIBAL. Cf. 204(U): STONE GIANT. Note that 144(U) has STUPID GIANT motif.
144(U). LOSS OF THE ANCIENTS

Corn Myths

5(M). CROW BRINGS CORN
29(M). Snow; loss of corn
67(U), 117(U). OFFENDED CORN SPIRIT
138(U). Origin of corn

Thunder Myths

53(U). Thunder wife
80(U?), 142(U). Thunder's Helper. Cf. 42(M), 139(U). Note that 42(M) and 139(U) include VOICE OF YOUNG THUNDER motif.
86(?), 202(U). SERPENT'S BRIDE. Cf. 143(U). Note that 202(U) includes Twelve women motif. Note that 86(?) includes modified VOICE OF YOUNG THUNDER motif.
140(U), 164(U), 178(U), 197(U). Man Who Visited the Thunders. Note that 164(U) includes VOICE OF YOUNG THUNDER motif.

Youthful Hero

43(M). Ganyo gowa (WHITE DEER)
54(U). White otter
57(U). Flute player returns to life
71(U). Ball player (THE BRIDE AND THE BROTHERS, with motifs TOOTHED BALL STICKS TO TREE and RESUSCITATION BY FRIGHTENING DEAD)

Bear Stories

60(U), 87(U), 116(U), 121(U), 122(M), 131(U), 174(U). BEAR BOY. Note that 60(U) and 87(U) open with abused-boy episode.
91(U?), 115(U). Bear Pet

Stars

12(?). Ursa Major legend
26(U), 80(U), 102(U), 103(U), 120(M), 123(M), 134(U). ORIGIN OF PLEIADES. Note that 80(U), 102(U), and 103(U) include TREE motif. Cf. Rising Star Children Hit by Clothes: 145(U), 157(U), 171(U), 185(U).

Visits to the Other World

4(M). Man near death visits the dead land. Cf. Visitor from sky world: 3(M).

6(Pontiac). Prophet brings new religion from heaven
13(?). Two men who visited the sky world, with RISING AND FALLING SKY motif.
74(M?). Visit to the dead
151(U), 194(U). DOG GUARDS ROUTE TO AFTERWORLD
163(U). ORPHEUS
200(U). MOTHER OF GHOSTS

Little People

70(U). Wemategunis. Cf. 55(U), 202(U).
132(U), 133(U). Woods dwarf (Matekanis, i.e., Wemategunis)

Punishments

55(U). Gambler punished
58(U). Ambitious eagle trapper punished
59(U). Hunter who neglects sacrifice to owl is punished
95(U). Animals punish woman who rejected men
126(U), 161(U), 216(U). PETITIONERS SELECT MAGICAL ATTRIBUTES with motif Would-be womanizer punished.
158(U). The Foolish Man

Relations with Other Tribes and Races

73(U), 172(U). Turtle Phratry Is Best. Cf. 62(U).
17(U?), 22(M), 28(M), 40(M), 83(U?), 203(U), 215(U). Arrival of the Dutch (with motif DIDO'S PURCHASE OF CARTHAGE). Note that 22(M) and 28(M) include motif LAND SALE WITH CHAIR DECEPTION; 28(M) and 40(M) include motif LIQUOR TRIED FIRST ON THE AGED. Cf. Arrival of the whites: 184(U).
31(Euro-American, several variants). Grasshopper War (TRIBES SEPARATE OVER TRIVIAL INCIDENT)
33(U), 37(U?), 213(U?). ORIGIN OF THE THREE RACES. Cf. 128(U), 135(U?).
63(U). Origin of alliance with Cherokees
85(U), 180(U). WHITE MAN CREATED FROM FOAM
98(U?). Treaty with the Dutch

101(M). Westward migration of the Munsees
118(M). Cattaraugus witch (TRIBES SEPARATE OVER TRIVIAL INCIDENT)
186(M). Snake Story

Ceremonial Origins

48(U), 88(U), 89(M), 96(U), 104(U), 113(U), 119(M). Origin of Big House. Note that 88(U) has motif SPLIT BODY IN SKY WORLD. Cf. 114(U). Also cf. Rising Star Children Hit by Clothes: 145(U), 157(U), 171(U), 185(U).
68(U?), 90(?), 94(U), 146(U). Origin of Doll Dance. Cf. 147(U), 207(U).
92(U), 100(U). Origin of Otter Ceremony
109–112(U). Origin of Peyote

Bible

27(U?), 35(U). FALL OF THE ANGELS
38(U?), 128(U), 183(U). DRUNKENNESS OF NOAH. Cf. ORIGIN OF THE THREE RACES.
81(U), 137(U), 199(U). TOWER OF BABEL. Note that 81(U) includes MIGRATION IN EXPANDING BOAT and MAGIC PARTING WATERS.
129(U). DANIEL IN THE LIONS' DEN
136(U). The earthquake and the dove (biblical DELUGE?). Cf. 9(U?).

Animal Tales

165(U), 177(U). Fox and rabbit
173(U), 210(U). Why rabbit's shoulders are narrow
188(M). Turtle discovers the earth is round
193(U). TURTLE WINS RACE
217(U). Why the crane has a long neck
218(U). Why the dove builds a nest the way he does

Dog Stories

130(U). Deserted boy and his dog
153(U). Dog eats at the table
196(U). How the dog became man's pet
151(U), 166(U), 175(U), 176(U). Dog who wanted to warm himself
159(U), 168(U), 179(U). WHY DOGS SNIFF ONE ANOTHER

Transformation Tales

105(M). Boy who turned into quails
206(U). Deer and peach tree
208(U). Screech-owl witch
209(U). Witch story (half dog, half man)

Miscellaneous

148(U), 189(U), 214(U). Mother-in-Law Story
190(U). Squirrel defies boy hunter
201(U). ETERNAL WEAVER; INEXHAUSTIBLE FOOD SUPPLY
205(U). Boy who couldn't hunt
212(U?). Three Rock Sisters

PART TWO : Story Abstracts

The abstracts are numbered in chronological order from A.D. 1655 to 1992. Following the abstract number: story title (if any) as given in the source; catchword, or descriptive name, in square brackets (underlined if there are Delaware variants, CAPITALIZED if there are variants outside Delaware tradition); source by author or by author and short title; the term "Munsee text" or "Unami text" if native-language text is included, usually with an English translation (trans.); date of collection (col.); date of publication (pub.); place of collection or place where informant lived; name of informant or tribe; total number of words in English; the abstract; miscellaneous notes.

In some cases (as with abstracts 3, 11, and 32), where the source is brief, the abstract is replaced by the complete English text, enclosed in quotation marks—but it may be noted that such sources are themselves synopses, or abstracts.

If the abstract number is preceded by an asterisk (*), the complete story may be read in the section Texts, this volume.

Throughout, Delaware folkloric motifs are underlined (e.g., Twelve women) and may be traced in Part One, above; more widespread motifs are capitalized (e.g., DELUGE) and may be traced in Part Four.

1650–1700

1. [Life of miracle worker]; Lindeström, ch. 15, pp. 208–9; col. ca. 1655; New Sweden; 250 words. A woman becomes pregnant by drinking from a creek and gives birth to a handsome, clever boy who performs "many miracles." When "somewhat" grown, the boy ascends to the sky, promising to return—but he never has. Later, another teacher, bearded and with a "large mouth" (like Europeans), comes among them, and he too ascends to the sky, promising to return; but he never has.

2. [TURTLE ISLAND with HUMANS CREATED FROM TREE]; Danckaerts, pp. 77–78, 175; col. 1679; Hackensack Munsee at site of present-day Bayonne per Goddard, "Ethnohistorical Implications"; Tantaqué, called Jasper; 250 words. At first there was only water; the tortoise raised its back,

water ran off, and "the earth became dry." A tree grew up in the middle of the earth; the first man sprouted from the tree's root, the first woman from the tip of the tree as it bent over and touched the earth.

3. [Visitor from sky world]; Wolley, p. 61; col. 1678–80; New York City area. "They have a Tradition . . . that about five hundred years agoe, a Man call'd (*Wach que ow*) came down from above, upon a Barrel's-head, let down by a Rope, and lived amongst them sixty years, who told them he came from an happy place, where there were many of their Nations, and so he left them."

4. [Man near death visits the dead land]; Wolley, p. 61; col. 1678–80; New York City area. "And they have another Tradition of one *Meco Nish,* who had lain as dead sixteen days . . . in which interval he told them he had been in a fine place where he saw all that had been dead."

5. [CROW BRINGS CORN]; Wolley, p. 42; col. 1678–80; New York City area. "They have a tradition that their Corn was at first dropt out of the mouth of a Crow from the Skies."

1760–1825

6. [Prophet brings new religion from heaven]; Williams, pp. 116–20; ca. 1763; Pontiac, but ostensibly derived from the Delaware Prophet, Neolin (see Leach, "Colonial Indian Wars," p. 141, and Hunter, "Delaware Nativist Revival"); 2,200 words. A Lenape man, eager to meet the Master of Life, travels eight days to a prairie, where he sees three paths. Fire turns him back from two of the paths. He takes the third path and finds a woman in white at a white mountain, who bids him bathe. After bathing, he climbs the mountain and proceeds to the handsomest of three villages. At the gate, the Master of Life bids him sit on a gold-bordered hat and instructs him to avoid liquor, polygamy, and "medicine song," which avoidance will enable him to live as Indians used to, without guns and European clothing. The French are to be tolerated; the English are to be driven away. The Indians are to recite a written prayer, which the Master of Life hands to the man. The woman in white leads him back to his home village; he must speak to no one until he sees the chief. To the chief he delivers the written prayer and the new laws.

7. [Origin of sand flies]; Heckewelder, *Narrative,* p. 121n; col. 1772; pertains to a place between Friedenshutten, i.e., Wyalusing on the Susquehanna, and the Muskingham country, toward which the Delawares were migrating; 100 words. Thirty years earlier (than 1772) a hermit magician dwelled on a certain rock, from which he would descend on travelers, frightening or murdering them. A "valiant chief" killed him, burned his bones to ashes, then threw them into the air, and they became sand flies (*ponksak*). The place in question was called Ponks Uteney (habitation of the sand fly, or gnat).

8. [Mammoth Legend]; Jefferson, p. 43; col. ca. 1780; Ohio per ibid., p. 208, but cf. p. 205 and note that the legend refers to Big Bone Lick (in Boone Co., Ky., per Silverberg, *Mammoths,* pp. 57, 76); 150 words. Mammoths were destroying game animals at the "Big bone licks." The "Great Man above" hurled thunderbolts at them from a neighboring mountain, killing all but one bull mammoth, who escaped and is still living north of the Great Lakes. *Note:* The story is retold in Richard Adams, *Legends of the Delaware Indians and Picture Writing,* without crediting Jefferson (see 47, below); reported as a "Shawnee" legend in Thomas Ashe's *Memoirs of Mammoth* . . . (1806), quoted in Schutz, "Study of Shawnee Myth," p. 14.

9. [DELUGE, EARTH DIVER]; Zeisberger, *History,* pp. 131–32; col. 18th c.; 170 words. After the DELUGE, survivors take refuge on a turtle's back. They ask the loon to dive for earth; it fails because the bottom is too deep, but then flies far and returns with earth in its bill (cf. biblical DELUGE). Guided by the loon, the turtle swims to dry land, and there the people settle.

10. [WOMAN WHO FELL FROM THE SKY, TWIN SONS]; Zeisberger, *History,* p. 132 (identified as Delaware in Loskiel, pt. 1, p. 24); col. 18th c. "Others . . . claim that the first human being fell from heaven. This was a woman cast out from the upper regions by her husband. Shortly after her fall from heaven she was delivered of twins, from whom the inhabitants of this land are descended."

11. [WOMAN WHO FELL FROM THE SKY, TWIN SONS, HARE AS DEMIURGE]; Zeisberger, *History,* p. 140; col. 18th c. "The hare is regarded as a great God and they bring offerings to it. The name of one of the twins born to the woman that was thrown from heaven was Tschimammus, that

is, hare. He made the land upon which the Indians dwell and was their ancestor. Now he is said to dwell in heaven, for many Indians who have been there have seen him and spoken to him and to them he has declared that he would come again." Cf. Loskiel, pt. 1, p. 40: "They sacrifice to an hare, because, according to [Zeisberger's?] report, the first ancestor of the Indian tribes had that name."

12. [Legend of Ursa Major]; Zeisberger, *History,* p. 148; col. 18th c.; 50 words. As paraphrased in Speck, *Big House,* p. 48: "Zeisberger relates the outline of a legend of the Bear group in which the Bear is pursued by Indians with a little dog; the three stars in the form of a triangle represent the head of a bear, which they cut from the trunk and threw down."

13. [Two men who visited the sky world]; Zeisberger, *History,* p. 147; col. 18th c.; 60 words. There is a place where the sky, moving up and down, strikes the water (or, according to some, a rock) (motif: RISING AND FALLING SKY). Two heroes set out to get through this opening; one of them succeeds, visits the sky world, and returns.

14. [WOMAN WHO FELL FROM THE SKY, TWIN SONS]; Loskiel, pt. 1, p. 24. "The Delawares say that the heavens are inhabited by men, and that the Indians descended from them to inhabit the earth: that a pregnant woman had been put away by her husband, and thrown down upon the earth, where she was delivered of twins, and thus by degrees the earth was peopled."

15. [WOMAN WHO FELL FROM THE SKY, TWIN SONS]; Bishop John Ettwein per Brinton, p. 132 (cf. p. 83); apparently 1788 per ibid., p. 132. First woman falls from heaven and bears twins. Belief: Benefactor would come from the east; thus newly arrived whites were considered divine.

16. [MIGRATION FROM THE WEST]; Heckewelder, *History,* ch. 1, pp. 47ff.; pub. 1819. The Lenni Lenape originally lived "in a very distant country in the western part of the American continent," migrated eastward to the Mississippi River, met the Mengwe (Iroquois), crossed through the country of the Talligewi (who were said to be giants), fought battles, and finally reached the Delaware-Hudson region.

17. [Arrival of the Dutch]; Heckewelder, *History,* ch. 2, pp. 71–75, 77, 262; pub. 1819; "taken down many years since from the mouth of an intelligent

Delaware"; 1,800 words. The Dutch arrived in what was perceived as a large fish or animal or house, and gave liquor, which was tried first by a brave chief; subsequently all were made drunk. The Dutch gave axes and other gifts; later they returned and laughed at the Indians for wearing the axes around their necks as ornaments. The Dutch spread a bull hide to show how much land they wished to acquire, then craftily cut the hide into a thin strip to encompass a large tract (cf. DIDO'S PURCHASE OF CARTHAGE).

18. [ANCESTORS EMERGE FROM UNDERWORLD]; Heckewelder, *History*, ch. 34, pp. 249–50, 253; pub. 1819; "Minsi" or "Monsey"; 220 words. At first, people lived in the earth under a lake. One man emerged through a hole and brought back a deer, which had been killed by a wolf. The people liked the meat so much that they emerged as a group. "The Unamis . . . and the Unalachtigos . . . have much similar notions, but reject the story of the lake, which seems peculiar to the Minsi tribe" (ibid., p. 250).

19. [GOLDEN AGE]; Heckewelder MS per Brinton, p. 135–36; 18th c. At first there was neither murder nor premature death, but (in Brinton's words) "this happy time was brought to a close by the advent of certain evil beings who taught men how to kill each other by sorcery."

20. [Earthly visit of "God" the teacher]; Luckenbach in Gipson, pp. 615–16; ca. 1805; White River, Ind.; 60 words. Once during a snowstorm God appeared from Heaven, wearing large snowshoes. After a long stay, during which he taught customs and "sacrificial feasts," he departed.

21. [ANCESTORS EMERGE FROM UNDERWORLD]; Trowbridge MS in Weslager, *History*, p. 474; 1823–24, White River, Ind.; Capt. Pipe of Sandusky per Kinietz, *Delaware Culture Chronology*, p. 79, or at least Pipe was Trowbridge's principal informant per ibid., p. 15–16; 150 words. Delawares are descendants of Wyandots, who sprang from a hole in the earth; the hole is "still to be seen on Lake Huron." A virgin gave birth to twins, a boy and a girl, who spoke a language different from Wyandot; these twins married and produced Delawares. Cf. "Origin of the Delawares" in Barbeau, *Huron and Wyandot Mythology*, p. 324: A headstrong Wyandot girl disobeys her father and flees with a lover of her own choosing; Delawares spring from this exiled couple.

22. [Arrival of the Dutch]; Trowbridge MS in Weslager, *History,* p. 475–76; 1823–24; Capt. Pipe; 600 words. Old man in the Big House prophesied the coming of "extraordinary events." Next day a ship arrived. Whites disembarked, and the Indians, thinking these were deities, spread skins for them to walk on. The whites offered liquor, which was tried first by three brave men. The whites asked for land the size of a bull's hide, then cut the hide into a cord to encompass a large area (cf. DIDO'S PURCHASE OF CARTHAGE); gave axes and hoes, which the Indians wore as necklaces. The whites bargained for more land, enough to hold their chair; but the chair seat was of cording, which, when unwound, encircled a large district (LAND SALE WITH CHAIR DECEPTION). After this, the Delawares vowed never again to grant land without an agreement on boundaries.

23. [Tradition of the great hunter Weekharmookhaas (Wehixamukes)]; Trowbridge MS in Weslager, *History,* p. 476; 1823–24; White River, Ind.; Capt. Pipe?; 200 words. There is a "long story" about this "great" man, who lived many ages past and generally hunted alone, traveling long distances. Men would get together to destroy him, but he would fly out the top of his wigwam and alight on a tree, would slay some with his club, then "dispatch the rest with contemptuous expressions to relate their fate." He had unlimited power among the people, and would kill the aged and infirm, telling them that they lived for nothing. See also the mention of a "great hunter" in ibid., p. 498.

24. [Tradition of chieftainship started by the Great Spirit]; Trowbridge MS in Weslager, *History,* p. 476; 1823–24; White River, Ind.; Capt. Pipe?; 70 words. The Great Spirit resided with humans in the beginning, then retired, telling them to depute a person with his, the Great Spirit's, qualities.

25. [CREATION BY THOUGHT]; Trowbridge MS in Weslager, *History,* p. 493; 1823–24; White River, Ind.; Capt. Pipe?; 120 words. The name Keshaalemookungk means "He who created us by this thought" (also mentioned in a narrative pub. 1808, quoted in Hunter, "Delaware Nativist Revival," where it is given as "keesh-she-la-mil-lang-up, or a being that thought us into being"). After the Creation, this supreme being remained on earth for a while, having "moral superintendency of all affairs." Then, having "perfected the system," he left. (Also: adherence to his instructions would lead to expulsion of the whites, per Hunter, loc. cit.)

26. [Myth of the seven stars, cf. ORIGIN OF THE PLEIADES]; "Answers to the questions," in Weslager, *Westward,* p. 110; ca. 1822; Ohio?, presumably from Unami sources (since the included word list is Unami per ibid., p. 135); 70 words. Seven boys are "afflicted by vomiting," and deprived of food until they become so much "like a deity" that they ascend to the sky.

27. [FALL OF THE ANGELS]; "Answers to the questions," in Weslager, *Westward,* p. 113; ca. 1822; Ohio?, from Unami sources? (see note to 26, above); 80 words. Devil refuses to acknowledge that the Creator has made all things, contending that he, the Devil, has made the bat (cf. GOOD AND EVIL CREATORS). In disgust the Devil plunges from heaven into the earth, where he remains.

28. [Arrival of the Dutch]; Cass-Trowbridge MS in Weslager, *Westward,* p. 165–70; 1821–22 per ibid., p. 163; evidently from Capt. Chipps; 200 words. A variant of the legend in Trowbridge MS (see 22, above); but here the liquor is tried first by two old men (LIQUOR TRIED FIRST ON THE AGED); and the LAND SALE WITH CHAIR DECEPTION precedes the bull-hide incident (DIDO'S PURCHASE OF CARTHAGE).

29. [The great snow and the famine]; Cass-Trowbridge MS in Weslager, *Westward,* pp. 170–71; 1821–22 per ibid., p. 163; Capt. Chipps?; 800 words. To make them realize their dependence upon him, the Great Spirit punishes the people with a deep snow and famine. Then, sent by the Great Spirit, an old man comes from the south with the gift of a magic oyster that need merely be attached to a tobacco pipe: whenever the pipe is knocked against the ice, another oyster appears. The old man leads a young person of the tribe to a hole in the sea ice, where the two descend to a large house and a former cornfield, meeting a certain woman. The old man and the child return to their people as the ice melts; the old man says, "Be glad and satisfied that I have returned—the Corn that has been so long lost is now returned to you—it appeared to me in the shape of a woman." Wild potatoes and much game are now available; corn is planted. People dance and worship the woman.

30. [WOMAN WHO FELL FROM THE SKY, EARTH DIVER, TURTLE ISLAND]; Cass-Trowbridge MS in Weslager, *Westward,* p. 182–83; 1821–22 per ibid., p. 163; Capt. Chipps?; 220 words. In the sky world, where there was a sunlike body called great cornstalk, a woman had a child; she was sick; she thought she could be cured if the cornstalk could be pulled up.

When it was pulled, there was total darkness. Vexed, the people threw the woman and her child down the hole where the cornstalk had been. The two were caught on the backs of hawks, who lowered them to the back of a turtle. A loon dived into the sea and brought back earth.

1850s

31. The Grasshopper War [TRIBES SEPARATE OVER TRIVIAL INCIDENT]; preserved only in Euro-American lore, in various late-19th-c. Pennsylvania versions compiled by Witthoft (see also Howard). Shawnee and Delaware children fight over a grasshopper; their mothers enter the fray, then the men join in. Many are killed. Thus Shawnees and Delawares become separate tribes.

32. [Origin of humans from thunder]; W. B. Parker, p. 683; pub. 1855; Texas. "The tradition of the Delawares, respecting their origin, is, that they sprung from a great eagle, who always hovers over them, and, when pleased, descends, and drops a feather; when displeased, he rises into the clouds and speaks in thunder. The feather is supposed to make the wearer invisible and invulnerable."

33. Origin of the Three Varieties of the Human Race [ORIGIN OF THE THREE RACES]; Morgan, *Journals,* p. 52; 1859; Kansas; "Delaware," i.e., Unami; 70 words. The black African was created first, a failure; the Great Spirit next created the Indian, an improvement; last, the white man. Cf. Gipson, pp. 344–45: first the African, then the Indian, last the white man (1805).

34. [Origin of Winter]; Morgan, *Journals,* p. 53; 1859; Kansas; "Delaware," i.e., Unami; 130 words. A married couple lived in the far north; they quarreled and the woman traveled southward. Lonely, the man went after her, carrying the cold with him. Every year he visits her. Cf. Harrington, *Religion,* pp. 25–26, for the Unami: winter and summer are caused by the *mani'towuk* of the north and the south playing a game of bowl and dice—the seasons are caused by their alternating fortunes.

35. [FALL OF THE ANGELS]; Morgan, *Journals,* p. 56; 1859; Kansas; "Delaware," i.e., Unami; 120 words. The Evil Spirit was created by the Good Spirit and was originally good; but when he caused contention among the lesser spirits, all took sides. The Good Spirit seized the Evil Spirit, tore off

one of his legs and replaced it with the leg of an ox, then sent him down to earth with the evil spirits who followed him.

36. [Origin of mosquitoes]; Morgan, *Journals*, p. 56; 1859; Kansas; "Delaware," i.e., Unami; 40 words. The wicked are punished after death by the Evil Spirit, who cuts their bodies to pieces. From these pieces spring mosquitoes and other noxious creatures.

37. [ORIGIN OF THE THREE RACES]; Gowing, pp. 2–3; ca. 1860?; Kansas; "Delaware," i.e., Unami?; 60 words. God made blacks first; thus they are called "the elder brother." "Not liking the color, He tried again, making one lighter, which is the Indian, then not satisfied, again He tried and the white man was the result and satisfactory."

38. [DRUNKENNESS OF NOAH]; Gowing, pp. 3–4; ca. 1860?; Kansas; "Delaware," i.e., Unami?. "When Noah was drunk his sons went in backward to cover him; Shem turned his head partly to look on him, which caused Shem to turn dark; Ham looked directly and was turned black, but Japheth did not look at all and retained his natural white skin: from the first came the Indian, from Ham the Negro. They also think the Negro was made to do the work, God giving them strength; to the Indian the bow and arrow and freedom, to the Whites books and wisdom."

39. [Origin of Winter]; Gowing, p. 4; ca. 1860?; Kansas; "Delaware," i.e., Unami?. "An old couple living in the north quarreled, and the wife went south; now and then the man relents and pays her a visit bringing along with him the north wind."

40. [Arrival of the Dutch]; Waubuno, pp. 3–4; pub. 1875?; Six Nations Munsee; 1,000 words. A prophet dreamed of white fog coming from the rising sun. Six years later a huge bird with white wings (i.e., a ship) arrived. Delawares thought it was the Great Spirit and spread thousands of beaver and otter skins for him to walk on. But the whites, instead of stepping on them, just admired them; they asked for land the size of a cowhide, and later cut the hide into strips to enclose a large area (cf. DIDO'S PURCHASE OF CARTHAGE). Whites gave axes, awls, knives, and rum. Delawares had old men try the rum, on the theory that the old were to die soon anyway (LIQUOR TRIED FIRST ON THE AGED). Thus "firewater" was introduced, and with it bloodshed. William Penn arrived and concluded a satisfactory treaty. The nine-article treaty is given in full.

1880–1900: Cattaraugus

41. Netyogwesûk [motif: Twelve women]; Curtin and Hewitt, NAA 3860, box 5, 5-page typescript labeled "1, Netyogwesûk, -16-, (modern), 5pp. 4to., (Delaware Story)"; since item 3860 is largely Cattaraugus Seneca folklore collected by Curtin in 1883, evidently with later annotations and additions by Hewitt, the included Delaware story could be as early as 1883, probably no later than Hewitt's Cattaraugus work of the 1890s; 850 words. "In the cliffs at the mouth of the Delaware R., on the right bank, were four openings in the rocks leading to the houses of twelve Netyogwesûk (Little Women)." These women quizzed each traveler on the river: if they received a kind answer, they let him pass; if unkind, they summoned their uncle, the great serpent, who came and ate the traveler, or they themselves would scalp him. Using the hair of the unkind travelers, they made bags with which they solicited fish offerings from fishermen. Ungenerous fishermen were punished with bad fishing luck. One youth dared to be swallowed by the serpent (JONAH motif), then cut himself free, killing the monster; afterward he set fire to the little women's houses. The little women tried to put out the blaze by urinating, but to no avail. By this time the people had all gathered on the opposite shore. The little women cursed them, warning of conquerors with "white eyes" who would drive the people away and make them poor.

42. Wíshakon and His Friend Visit the Pléthoak (Thunders) [cf. Thunder's Helper]; Curtin, *Seneca Myths,* pp. 206–10, cf. Curtin and Hewitt, "Seneca Fiction," no. 28: The Old Man and the Boy; 1883; Cattaraugus, a "Delaware story told by John Armstrong"; 1,500 words. An old man and a boy called Wíshakon live together. They go off to see the world, taking a canoe to an island. A well-dressed stranger comes for them and leads them to the lodge of the Thunders, where they are asked to help kill the Thunders' enemies. The boy, who has great power, kills (1) a giant porcupine, (2) a sunfish, and (3) a disease-bearing creature that flies and is "as big as a cloud." The old man returns home, but Wíshakon joins the Thunders and travels with them. "After the great Thunders roar we hear the little fellow with his alto voice" (motif: VOICE OF YOUNG THUNDER).

43. The Ganyo Gowa (Great Game, i.e., WHITE DEER); Curtin, *Seneca Myths,* pp. 156–59 (of which another, similar version is in Curtin and Hewitt, NAA 3860, box 2, booklet with cover sheet inscribed "Armstrong Nov. 1883," pp. 67–71), cf. Curtin and Hewitt, "Seneca Fiction," no. 110;

1883; Cattaraugus, "a Delaware story told by John Armstrong"; 1,200 words. An old man tells his grandson that the boy's parents were killed when going toward the "ganyo gowa." Seeking revenge, the boy travels to a lake and kills a swan; but the grandfather is not satisfied. The grandfather now says the parents were killed by creatures in a certain "wizard spring." The boy goes there, loses both legs, gets them back, burns up the creatures, and proceeds to a lodge with owl sentinels. Inside is an old man asleep with a white deer in his bosom. The boy transfers the deer to his own bosom and flees, followed by all the animals (the white deer is the master of game). The sleeping man, who is brother to the boy's grandfather, wakes and pursues the boy, pounds the boy's head, and retrieves the white deer. The boy in turn pursues the old man, kills him, takes the deer back, and goes home. The grandfather, angry because his brother has been killed, sticks arrows in the boy's back. The boy kills the grandfather, then travels west with the white deer, followed by all the game in the world; he meets a boy who becomes his friend. The two boys decide to live together and liberate the white deer. From that time on, animals have roamed the world. *Note:* "The Indians call a white deer the king of the deer and believe that the rest flock about and follow him" (Zeisberger, *History,* p. 64).

44. The Legend of Moskim [WOMAN WHO FELL FROM THE SKY, TURTLE ISLAND, TWIN SONS]; Curtin, NAA 2204, Munsee text and trans.; col. 1883; Cattaraugus; John Armstrong; 600 words. A husband in the sky world is jealous of the "comet." When the sky tree is uprooted, the husband pushes his pregnant wife through the hole. As she falls, she grabs a handful of earth with huckleberry bushes; the comet hands her seed corn, a kettle, a beaver bone, a mortar, and a pestle. As she falls toward the water below, the pike offers to support her; but the manitos (manitous) only ridicule him. The turtle is chosen to support her. Her child is born; she spreads the earth on the turtle's back. In time her child, a daughter, is impregnated by wind and gives birth to twin sons, Flint and Moskim ("rabbit" or "hare") (HARE AS DEMIURGE). Flint exits through his mother's navel, killing her. The grandmother buries the mother with her head to the west, thus establishing the path of souls, who travel westward after death.

45. [WOMAN WHO FELL FROM THE SKY, TURTLE ISLAND, TWIN SONS]; Hewitt, NAA 16, Munsee text and partial trans.; col. 1896; Cattaraugus; John Armstrong; 1,000 words. Fuller version of the preceding, with these additional details: before the pike offers to be the earth supporter, the sunfish volunteers; both are rejected as too ugly; the turtle is chosen, because

it is "strong"; the woman creates the sun, also the "bear chasers" (Ursa Major) and the "dancers" (Pleiades); her daughter plays by bouncing up and down on a branch, then prostrates herself and is impregnated by wind. Again the twins are Flint and Moskim (HARE AS DEMIURGE).

46. [WOMAN WHO FELL FROM THE SKY, TURTLE ISLAND, TWIN SONS, DYING BROTHER]; Hewitt, "Iroquoian Cosmology," first part, p. 221–54; 1896; Cattaraugus; John Armstrong; 5,000 words. A yet fuller version of the preceding two stories (with slightly different details), translated by Hewitt from Armstrong's narration in the Seneca language. Here the elder of the twins is not named. No mention of the name Moskim.

1900–1915

47. The Legend of the "Yáh Qúa W'hee" or Mastodon [Mammoth Legend]; Richard Adams, *Delaware Indian Legend*, pp. 71–72; pub. 1899; Adams claims he has never seen this story published, but it is suspiciously similar to the version in Jefferson (see 8, above); 530 words. Mastodons, placed on earth as beasts of burden, made war on the other animals. The Great Spirit decided they must be annihilated. Thus all men and animals warred against the mastodons until there was so much blood that the mastodons became mired, sank, and died. The scene of this battle was the Ohio Valley. One last bull mastodon escaped to the far north. Today the mastodons' bones are found in marshes. In remembrance of the battle and to compensate for the food animals that lost their lives warring against the mastodons, the Great Spirit caused the cranberry to grow as food in the marshes, blood-red in commemoration.

48. [Origin of Big House]; Richard Adams, *Ancient Religion*, pp. 8–17; pub. 1904; Okla.?; 1,800 words. When the Delawares lived in the Delaware Valley, they became so rich and powerful that they forgot to give thanks to the Creator. There were natural upheavals: drought, famine, earthquake; mountains reared up, streams appeared in dry places. At this time a mistreated boy was sent to dig wild sweet potatoes. He brought back many, but when the people cooked them, they gave the boy nothing. Starving, the boy cried to the Great Spirit, "O-oo," and heard twelve echoes. In his sleep a spirit with a face half red came to him, instructed him in rites of the Thanksgiving Dance, and showed him how to build the "large house" with a center post "with four faces carved on it." Extensive ceremonial details are given.

49. The Story of Wa-e-aqon-oo-kase [Wehixamukes]; Richard Adams, *Legends,* pp. 7–15; pub. 1905; E. Okla.?; 2,900 words. W, an orphan, was mistreated by an old couple. They starved him, insulted him, and made him work. But a spirit came to him and promised him a "charmed life." Often he accompanied hunters and warriors as a servant.

One time the hunters told W to go on ahead and mix meal at a certain water hole. Taking the instruction literally, he mixed meal *in* the water hole.

The hunters mentioned, "It would be nice if we had a turkey to dip in this lard." W caught a live turkey and dipped it in the lard.

W joined the other men in a bear hunt and responded to the instruction "Call out when you see a hole in a tree" by pointing out a woodpecker hole.

They told him to go on ahead and look for a smooth, level place to make a campfire. He made it on a frozen lake.

Once, while on a war party, he fooled the enemy by placing a blood-spattered bladder on his own head, as if he had been scalped. When the enemy approached, he jumped up and killed them.

Another time, however, he was placed as sentinel beside his hidden tribesmen (who had buried themselves in sand) with instructions to "see that the enemy passed over them." The enemy in fact passed around them, so W called them back and told them to pass *over* them—much to the annoyance of W's fellow warriors.

When he had grown, people often warned disobedient children that W would carry them off. Which he did, so as not to make liars of the parents.

When he was old, living with his wife, he defeated a party of enemies by hurling scalding hominy at them.

When he was very old, he went out with his wife to cut down a tree. As it fell, he sprang toward it, as if to catch it, and vanished. His voice said he would return to help the Delawares when they needed him to fight battles.

50. [Wehixamukes and his nephew]; Adams, *Legends,* p. 16; pub. 1905; E. Okla.?; 400 words. W had a nephew who, like W, was a gifted man. Once, when they camped in a party, they built a fire against an old tree, recalling the saying that a tree when it falls will strike the bravest. During the night the tree fell toward the nephew, arousing W's envy. This led to a deadly feud between the two, but they became friends again.

Another time, W and his nephew set off to go around the world and came to a country of giants, who terrified W. But W's nephew helped him to jump from hill to hill until they got home safely. Cf. Speck's notes on "the boy," who was foolish but second in power to W, often surpassing him (War Eagle, Letters, p. 111).

51. The Story of Kup-ah-weese [FORTUNATE HUNTER]; Adams, *Legends,* pp. 20–23; pub. 1905; W. Okla.?; 1,500 words. Two episodes about a lazy, worthless, but good-natured drunkard:

K brags that he will kill his only cow to feast the tribe (thus thoughtlessly impoverishing himself and his wife). When the cow is killed, it is found to have swallowed a fancy coat with $100 worth of silver buttons—which K uses to make his wife an excellent dress.

Having squandered everything, K asks his wife for chicken soup. But there is no chicken. Then he goes fishing, catches a turkey with his fishline; sees geese in the water and ties them; they fly carrying him along (motif: FORTUNATE HUNTER FLIES WITH GEESE); geese catch in a tree, strangling a raccoon. K drops into the river, lands on a huge fish (thus accidently killing the fish), brings home turkey, geese, and raccoon to his wife; together they come back to get the fish, which, as they discover when they cut it open, has swallowed a bear. Thus they have plenty of meat for the season.

52. The Legend of the Great Bear; Adams, *Legends,* p. 34; pub. 1905; Okla.?; 350 words. The great bear was grandfather of all the bears; lived in the Alleghenies. Children were told the great bear would catch them. Finally the bear was wounded in battle with the mastodon. Directed by the Great Spirit, a hunter went and extracted its "tusk" (i.e., tooth), which thereafter served as a medicine charm.

53. The Story of Hingue-kee-shu: Bigmoon Afterwards Rainmaker; Adams, *Legends,* pp. 36–38; pub. 1905; Okla.?; 800 words. A lost youth named Hingue-kee-shu lived for twenty years with the Pate-hock-hoo-ees, or rain spirits. After returning home, he was loved by a maiden. But he had a wife among the rain spirits, who jealously sent a storm. Thus the man had to renounce mortal love. While he lived, the people always had rain; he became known as Sa-soo-a-lung-hase, or Rainmaker.

54. The Story of Mek-ke-hap-pa; Adams, *Legends,* pp. 39–44; pub. 1905; Okla.?; 2,500 words. A Chief named Sax-kees promises that the man who can kill a certain white otter may choose one of his six daughters for a bride. A poor, scabby youth named Mek-ke-hap-pa succeeds, but the chief

merely gives him his eldest daughter, with no choice. The youth now appears healthy and handsome in fine furs provided by his grandmother. Famine punishes the chief, who sends his principal servant, known as the Puchel, to summon Mek-ke-hap-pa to be chief in his place; he also gives him the remaining five daughters.

55. Che-py-yah-poo-thwaw; Adams, *Legends,* pp. 45–46; pub. 1905; Okla.?; 700 words. A handsome youth with beautiful eyes entices all the other youths to become gamblers and forget their duties as hunters and warriors. To teach him a lesson, the great Chief of the gamblers, Che-py-yah-poo-thwah, who lives in the moon, comes to earth and gambles with the youth, winning his eyes. A little boy called Way-mah-tah-kun-eese (Wemategunis) goes to the sky world and retrieves the eyes from an old lady who is wearing them as a necklace at a great dance; the little boy restores the youth's eyes in exchange for the promise that he will quit gambling.

56. The Battle With the Monster; Adams, *Legends,* pp. 49–50; pub. 1905; Okla.?; 700 words. Men and animals ganged up on the grandfather of the monsters; they scattered his brains and each took some. The monster's brains contained all qualities, and the men and animals scrambled carelessly for their share; thus, animals got some strange attributes, and men, having gotten a mixture of all, are changeable.

57. Wa-sha-xnend or The Man They Cannot Hold; Adams, *Legends,* pp. 51–54; pub. 1905; Okla.?; 1,350 words. A gifted youth who plays flute has as his guardian an evil water manitou that lives in a cave beneath the surface of the river. The youth attracts women, arousing jealousy in other men, who finally appoint a sorceress to kill him. When he is dead, his old mother throws him into the river; he returns to life after six days.

58. The Warrior and the Eagle; Adams, *Legends,* pp. 55–57; pub. 1905; Okla.?; 750 words. An ambitious eagle trapper rejects ordinary eagles. To punish him, the outsized blood-red grandfather of the eagles carries him to its nest and holds him prisoner awhile.

59. The Hunter and the Owl; Adams, *Legends,* pp. 58–60; pub. 1905; Okla.?; 700 words. An unlucky hunter prays to an owl for success, promising to give it some fat and a heart. But when he kills a deer, he neglects the promised sacrifice. The owl reappears and curses him; the hunter then curses the owl. Worried, they both call off their curses, and the hunter

hangs out the sacrifice. All is well. Cf. Loskiel, pt. 1, pp. 44–45: sacrifice to owl brings hunting success.

60. The Little Boy and the Bears [BEAR BOY]; Adams, *Legends,* pp. 61–63; pub. 1905; E. Okla.?; 1,000 words. An orphan lives with his uncle and the uncle's cruel wife; the wife promises the boy bear fat but merely gives him foam skimmed from hominy. Saddened by the boy's plight, the uncle puts him "out of his misery" by imprisoning him in a cave behind a boulder. Inside, the boy spends the winter with a bear and a porcupine. In the spring, the boy is adopted by a mother bear with cubs. They live in a hollow tree. A hunter comes and kills all except the boy and one cub. When the cub is grown, it is released. The boy becomes a great warrior.

61. A-le-pah-qua: The Woman with the Two Plants [Origin of love medicine]; Adams, *Legends,* pp. 64–65; pub. 1905; Okla.?; 871 words. A manitou gave a certain woman two plants, explaining a ritual to attract the opposite sex. Thus the woman had power over men. The secret was passed from daughter to daughter.

62. The Clans [Turtle Phratry Is Best]; Adams, *Legends,* pp. 66–68; pub. 1905; Okla.?; 120 words of English verse. The turtle saved people from a great DELUGE; those saved became the Turtle clan. The Wolf clan is descended from children nursed by a wolf, whose wailing called hunters to come aid the babies. The Turkey clan is descended from a maiden who had a vision of a turkey that would sound an alarm to warn warriors when the enemy was near.

63. The Legend of Alliance of the Delawares and Cherokees; Adams, *Legends,* pp. 72–75; pub. 1905; E. Okla.?; 1,500 words. In the old country the Cherokees challenged the Delawares to a contest with their reputed strong man. The Delawares sent forth their conjurer, Po-con-gui-gu-la, who overmastered the Cherokee and arranged a truce. Years later, when the Cherokees were besieged by Osages out west, they sent to Indiana for Delaware aid, which was forthcoming. Forty years later the Delawares and Cherokees drew up a written pact; hence the beginning of Delaware residence in Oklahoma Cherokee territory.

64. [Origin of rain-making charm, cf. The Water Monster and the Sun]; Harrington, "Some Customs," p. 58; pub. 1910; E. Okla.?; 50 words. On the shores of the Big Water Where Daylight Appears some heroes cap-

tured the Horned Serpent and took scales from its back. These are kept in a pouch and used as rain charm.

65. [DELUGE, EARTH DIVER, TURTLE ISLAND]; Harrington, "Sketch," p. 232–33; pub. 1913; Okla.; 120 words. After the Great Spirit created the world, he flooded it (some Munsee say it was Nanapush, but other Munsee say this is Ojibwa influence); then he sent various animals diving to bring up earth. At last the muskrat succeeded, placing earth on the turtle's back, which increased in size. *Note:* Newcomb, p. 72, n. 96, says his informant Martha Bob "related essentially the same myth."

66. A Youth and His Uncle; Prince, "Modern Delaware Tale," Munsee text and trans. (poetic version in Leland and Prince, pp. 256–59); pub. 1902; Hagerstown Munsee, Chief Nelles Montour (see Leland and Prince, pp. 31–33); 650 words. A youth makes a down-lined basket for his dying uncle to lie in and angrily sends away the cannibal death spirit Muttóntoe, who vows to return. The youth goes west, meets an odd-looking small boy (cf. Wemategunis), seeks advice from an old wizard, and returns home. He then puts his uncle in his own bed, and lies in the basket that he had made for the uncle. When Muttóntoe comes, the youth springs up all covered with feathers, frightening Muttóntoe away.

*67. Disappearance of Mother Corn [OFFENDED CORN SPIRIT]; Harrington, Papers, OC-161:1; col. 1907–10; E. Okla.; Charles Elkhair; 750 words. Young boys doubted corn was a living spirit. Then "the heart of Corn turned into living beings [evidently weevils], and all began disappearing in flight with wings." Mesingw came to warn the people that an offense had been committed. Two poor boys traveled to the sky world, and found Mother Corn all scabby because people had parched their corn without using tallow. She agreed to return after they made a sacrifice of burnt mussel shells.

68. [Origin of Doll Dance]; Harrington, *Dickon,* p. 80; col. 1907–10?; pub. 1938; E. Okla.; 260 words. A little girl had a doll her father had made for her, but she treated it so much like a real baby and spent so much time with it that her parents worried and finally made her throw it away. She became sick and dreamed about the doll, which instructed her in certain rites.

69. Origin of Stories; Harrington, Papers, OC-160:1, retold in *Dickon,* pp. 287–88; col. 1907–10; Okla.?; 120 words. A hunter in the woods hears a

little voice singing. The sound comes from a small hole in the ground. The creature tells stories in exchange for a gift of tobacco or a piece of bread. This is the origin of stories.

*70. Wēmatē′gŭnīs (He is everywhere) [i.e., Wemategunis]; Harrington, Papers, OC-160:1, retold in *Dickon,* pp. 288–89; col. 1907–10; E. Okla.; Julius Fouts; 200 words. A hunter kills a deer, then calls to his friends. Hearing a voice across the hollow, he runs to it, calls again, hears a voice from where he has just come—and discovers a little man with a little bow, who has thus tricked him. He challenges the little man to a fight. But the little one takes off twelve cornhusk jackets in succession, growing smaller each time, until he is so small the hunter is ashamed to fight him. Instead he gives the little man the name "Answer-me" and sends him home.

71. Ball Player [THE BRIDE AND THE BROTHERS]; Harrington, Papers, OC-163:9 (MS), typescript in Papers, OC-161:1, retold in *Dickon,* pp. 290–97; col. 1909; E. Okla.; Julius Fouts; 2,400 words. The eldest of six brothers weds a maiden with blue and green hair, who is promptly stolen by the evil Red-Feather-on-His-Head. One after another the brothers try to rescue the maiden, but each is killed by the *yahquaha,* the pet of Red-Feather. As each is killed, the remaining brothers at home see blood appear on a flute. Finally the youngest, called Ball Player—his "ball" is a wildcat skull (motif: TOOTHED BALL STICKS TO TREE)—sets out, aided by the skull and four other animal helpers (otter, fire toad, snake, and weasel). He kills the *yahquaha,* incinerates Red-Feather, and revives his five dead brothers (shooting an arrow into the air for each one, calling "Look out!") (motif: RESUSCITATION BY FRIGHTENING DEAD). All six brothers, along with the eldest's wife, return home.

72. The Snow Boy [Snow Boy]; Harrington, Papers, OC-163:9; col. 1907–10; probably E. Okla.; 300 words. A girl gives birth to a strange boy who sucks other children's fingers, turning the fingers black and stiff as if frozen. When a little older, he has his mother leave him on an ice floe. Thus he departs, promising to return with snow for hunters to track game. Thereafter the people leave a miniature canoe filled with sweetened parched corn at the river's edge as an offering for Snow Boy.

*73. Why the Turtle Phratry Is Best [Turtle Phratry Is Best]; Harrington, Papers, OC-163:9; col. 1907–10; Okla.?; 140 words. The three totem animals—Turtle, Wolf, and Turkey—once had an argument as to which was best. As they argued, they came to a river, on the other side of which was food. Turkey boasted he could get to it, but flew and fell short. Wolf could only pace back and forth on the river bank. Turtle swam underwater and got it. Thus Turtle is best, next Turkey, last Wolf. *Note:* According to Heckewelder, *History,* p. 253, the Turtle "tribe" is best because the turtle supports the earth; Zeisberger, *History,* p. 131, gives a deluge myth in which the Turtle tribe is "most important" because it repeopled the earth; Weslager *History,* p. 292, citing *Pennsylvania Colonial Records,* tells how the Turtle group gained its superior position in the late 18th century (when other chiefs ceded authority to the Turtle chief).

*74. A Visit to the Land of Spirits; Harrington, Papers, OC-163:9; col. before 1910?; 180 words. A few "Minsi" men travel southwest to see where the dead go, come to a deserted village where people appear at nightfall, talking, laughing, and drumming. One of the men takes a fancy to one of the women. When his companions set off for home, this man kills himself so he can stay with the woman.

*75. Cyclone; Harrington, Papers, OC-163:9; col. before 1907–10?, Okla.?; 150 words. A man went hunting with his little boy, who was "old enough to cook and watch horses." Cyclone carried off the camp and the boy; it "was a person walking on his hands, with his feet in the air; he had long hair trailing the ground." The man caught up with it and threatened to kill this cyclone person. But it saved its life by relinquishing the boy and the camp.

76. [The sun and the cornbread]; Harrington, Papers, OC-163:9; col. 1907–10?; Okla.?; 150 words. The sun, Ki'co, is a man who travels all day across the sky. Once at night a man came into the house and asked a woman for bread. She had none; but he kept insisting. Finally he reached out and picked up a piece of cornbread and cut it into four quarters; blood came out. He ate the bread. Thereafter, whenever the woman had a child it died right away. "The sun had made his bread out of something that ought to have remained to give life to the children."

77. [EARTH DIVER, TURTLE ISLAND]; Harrington, Papers, OC-163:9; col. before 1907–10?; Okla.? "The earth is flat and is supported beneath by a great mud turtle which carries the earth on his back. The muskrat began to build the earth in the first place, when everything was water, on top of a big mud turtle. And then the beavers came and carried more earth then."

*78. A Delaware Snake Legend [cf. THE HUNTERS AND THE WATER MONSTER]; Harrington, Papers, OC-163:9; col. 1907–10; E. Okla; Julius Fouts; 370 words. Twelve men were out hunting. One of them heard a turkey gobbling, went to investigate, and never returned. Next day a second man disappeared the same way. Later they discovered a huge serpent in a tree, gobbling; then it slid into the water. People sang nightly to raise the creature. They raised a great fish, also "a large turtle with trees growing on its back" (motif: FISHED-UP TURTLE, cf. motif TURTLE ISLAND). Finally they raised the great snake, burned its body, and each took a piece of the bone to use as medicine.

*79. Strong Man [Wehixamukes]; Harrington, Papers, OC-163:9; col. 1907–10?; E. Okla.?; 900 words. A tale made up of several episodes: (1) while on the warpath, the strong man sleeps in camp; (2) he alerts the enemy; (3) he defeats the enemy single-handedly, mutilating the sole survivor; (4) he finds a "bear" hole but is mistaken; (5) when his companions have found the bear, he pushes it out of its hole; (6) he dips a live turkey in bear grease; (7) told to "kill the first thing you see," he kills two men. The narrator concludes: "And afterwards, he always went by himself anyplace. They wouldn't say anything to him."

*80. Seven Stars [Thunder's Helper and ORIGIN OF PLEIADES with TREE motif]; Harrington, Papers, OC-163:9; col. before 1910; Okla.?; 400 words. There were eight boys, of whom seven could rise into the air or sink into the earth. The eighth could not. Giving up on him, his grandfather marooned him on an island. A horned serpent offered to ferry him to shore if he would look out for thunderclouds. The boy betrayed him to the Thunders, and the serpent was struck just as the boy landed safely on the mainland. The Thunders then befriended the boy. The other seven boys turned into red stones. But a thoughtless man defiled the stones, which turned into seven pines. At last, when too many people came and lay in their shade, they rose to become the Pleiades.

81. Story of Origin [TOWER OF BABEL, MIGRATION ACROSS OCEAN, MAGIC PARTING OF WATERS]; Harrington, Papers, OC-161:1; col. 1907–10?; Okla.?; 200 words. Version A: At first all people were the same; there were no whites, blacks, or Indians; while building a big house that would keep them safe from the DELUGE, people suddenly noticed they were speaking different languages; Delawares came away, parted the ocean waters, and arrived in America; the waters closed on their ene-

mies. Version B: Shawnees came over as described above for the Delawares; Delawares crossed in a magic canoe that expanded to hold them all [MIGRATION IN EXPANDING BOAT].

82. The Lost Boy; Harrington, Papers, OC-161:1; col. 1907–10; Okla.?; 450 words. A boy is sucked up by a great wave in the river; his father seeks the advice of a mystic and then goes to the mouth of the river, where he sees his son with a beautiful "mermaid." The son cannot now return.

83. Ma Ha X Ci Gun (White Man) [Arrival of the Dutch]; Harrington, Papers, OC-161:1; col. before 1910?; 300 words. Seven years before the whites came, a prophet had sung a riddle song: "I saw somebody smoking, he had a knife in his hand, he was swimming on his back." Whites arrived with a gift of hoes, axes, dishes; took a Delaware girl as bride; returned a year later with the young woman's child. Delawares hung the implements around their necks. Whites cheated the Delawares in a land sale, using a bull hide (cf. DIDO'S PURCHASE OF CARTHAGE).

*84. The Big Fish [The Water Monster and the Sun]; Harrington, Papers, OC-161:1; col. before 1907–10?; Okla.?; 850 words. A little girl becomes pregnant while playing near a creek and gives birth to a fish. Her grandmother puts the fish in a water-filled impression left by a horse's hoof. Both the fish and the impression increase in size until they become a man-eating monster in a large lake. Two boys then change into birds and fly to the sun, who gives them ashes. They return to the lake, where one boy becomes a butterfly and goes underground beneath the lake; the other boy turns into "a sun" and positions himself above the water. Both deposit ashes, which dry up all the water, killing the fish. When their deed is discovered, they are rewarded with wampum. Before this, "the boys had to parch corn and eat it by the fire, but now they live good and have plenty."

*85. Creation of the White Man [WHITE MAN CREATED FROM FOAM]; Harrington, Papers, OC-161:1; col. 1907–10; E. Okla.; Julius Fouts; 650 words. Created from river foam by a stranger whom God sent to earth, the white man was taught arts by the stranger's brother, the Devil.

86. The Girl Who Joined the Thunders [SERPENT'S BRIDE with modified VOICE OF YOUNG THUNDER]; Harrington, Papers, OC-161:1; col. before 1907–10?; Okla.?; 600 words. A certain young woman would not marry;

finally she was wooed by a handsome stranger, who took her to his home beneath the water. While he was out hunting, she found his serpent suit. She fled, he pursued. Her dream helper, the weasel, entered the serpent-man through his throat and cut out his heart. The girl reached the shore, where the Thunders were waiting for her. They rubbed her body, and little snakes dropped out. She went to live with the Thunders, saying, "When a cloud comes up making a continual rolling or rumbling sound, that is the noise made by my garments."

87. Rock-Shut-Up [BEAR BOY]; Harrington, Papers, OC-160:1; col. 1907–10?; Okla.; 1,800 words. A boy's uncle shuts him up in a hole, using a rock—at the behest of his wife, who hates the nephew. A buffalo tries to push the rock aside. A bear succeeds, and gives the boy to a female bear, who raises him with her two cubs. Boy and cubs go pecan gathering and play a trick on some old bears: they make noises like dogs and hunters, scare off the oldsters, and steal their pecans. One day a light appears at the door of their tree den; the mother bear "licks the light off," saying, "They [the hunters] will not find us now." But one day the light persists and a hunter arrives. The mother tells the boy to go first, so they will not be killed. But he refuses. The mother and the male cub are killed. Finally the boy emerges; he and the female cub are spared; a tobacco offering is tied around the female cub's neck. Now the boy has hunting power. Bears call him A-sun-Ke-pon, i.e., Rock-Shut-Up. *Addendum in a different hand:* The boy abuses bears: wounds them and lets them go. In revenge they lure him, using a little bear who wears a bigger bear's "shoes" (so the tracks will be more enticing to the young hunter). The hunter is thus led into an ambush; the bears knock off his arms and legs, mend him, and send him back home to tell what has happened. When he arrives home, his arms and legs drop off again. *Note:* The name Rock-Shut-Up appears in a 19th-c. Delaware census (per Rementer, Letters on Delaware Folklore, 11 May 1990).

88. Origin of the Mask, and of the Big House [motif: SPLIT BODY IN SKY WORLD]; Harrington, *Religion,* pp. 147–51; pub. 1921; E. Okla.; Charles Elkhair; 750 words. One of three abandoned boys is taken to the rocky mountains in the sky by *Mĭsinghâli'kŭn,* who promises him strength and power. Later, while hunting, the boy sees *Mĭsinghâli'kŭn* riding a buck, herding the other deer. Thereafter, people abandon the Big House (reason not given), which in those days had no faces of the *Mĭsi'ng*ʷʿ. But after ten

years a twelve-month earthquake comes "because they had abandoned the worship." *Mĭsinghâli'kŭn* reappears and instructs the people in a new form of worship. Cf. Origin of Big House.

89. [Origin of Munsee Big House ceremony: Origin of Big House]; Harrington, *Religion,* pp. 127–28; pub. 1921; Six Nations Munsee; 110 words. The Great God came down to earth and told the people what to do; then, carrying twelve shining sticks of sumac, which he dropped to earth one by one, he disappeared in the heavens with a crash like thunder. Thereafter they held the Big House meetings as he had instructed them.

90. [Origin of Doll Dance]; Harrington, *Religion,* pp. 162–63; pub. 1921; Okla.?; 200 words. Children made dolls that "seemed to have life." Disturbed, their parents ordered them to throw the dolls away. But one little girl dreamed of the doll she had made, which instructed her to retrieve it and hold a ceremony for good health.

91. [Bear Pet]; Harrington, *Religion,* p. 172; pub. 1921; Okla.?; A certain family kept a bear cub as pet. When it was grown, they released it with a tobacco gift. Afterward their little boy fell sick. An Indian doctor told the parents to hold a ceremony, to be repeated every two years. Thus the child recovered and kept his health.

92. [Origin of Otter Ceremony]; Harrington, *Religion,* pp. 176–79; pub. 1921; Okla.?; 280 words. A girl, realizing that the pet otter she had raised was "pure," or "sacred," tied a tobacco bag to its neck and released it into the wild. Later the girl became sick because her pet otter "wanted something to eat." People held a hog feast "in the name of the otter." Subsequently the feast was kept up for "the health of all."

*93. [THE TURTLE WHO CARRIED THE PEOPLE]; Michelson, NAA 2776, f. 3; col. 1912 or 1913; Okla.; 1,100 words. A gang of twelve outlaws came upon a giant turtle and decided to ride it in order to save walking. When the turtle headed for the "big water," the men found they were stuck fast. Just one of them managed to get off before it submerged. He returned to his Delaware tribesmen, and they all went to the Shawnee for a "medicine" that would help rescue the missing eleven. This was brought to the shore, and by means of it they began to summon the turtle. But other water animals, including a crayfish and a monster serpent, came one after another.

At last the turtle (FISHED-UP TURTLE) appeared with the men, who were thus rescued.

*94. Doll Dance [Origin of Doll Dance]; Michelson, NAA 2776, f. 4; col. 1912 or 1913; Okla.; 2,000 words. Parents gave their little girls rags to use in making dolls, but one girl preferred to play with a stick that resembled a human. Fearing this, her parents made her throw it away. Subsequently it appeared in the girl's dreams, threatening to choke her. She fell sick. Doctors discovered that the doll had caused the illness. They ordered the girl's parents to make a special doll and hold an annual dance in its honor. Extensive ceremonial details are given.

*95. [The woman who rejected men, with motif WOMAN WHO REFUSES TO MARRY]; Michelson, NAA 2776, f. 5, Unami text and trans.; col. 1912; Okla.; 470 words. A good-looking woman who rejects men is courted by beaver, skunk, and owl, each of whom she also rejects, calling them ugly. Beaver tricks her by gnawing a log bridge; when she has fallen into the water, she calls to the three animals for help. They ignore her, and she drowns.

*96. Delaware Meetinghouse [Origin of Big House]; Michelson, 2776, f. 10; col. 1912; Okla.; 3,500 words. The Delawares received the Big House when God gave "churches" to all "nations." But the Delawares neglected the meetings during a protracted war. As a result the earth shook for a year. Trees sank. Pools of water appeared. To "check this," they held meetings in a makeshift Big House of two bark lodges put together. There was no regular meetinghouse. After six months, the earth began to stop shaking. A regular Big House, with spirit faces, was set up. The faces spoke, giving instructions for conducting the ritual. Extensive ceremonial details are given.

*97. Wehīx̄amōkäs the Delaware Sampson [Wehixamukes]; Michelson, NAA 2776, f. 9; col. 1912; Okla.; Silas Longbone(?) or Charles Elkhair(?); 3,200 words. Epic of numerous episodes:

While on the warpath, he sleeps in camp.
He alerts the enemy.
He defeats enemy single-handedly; mutilates sole survivor.
He finds a "bear" hole but is mistaken.

Others find bear; he pushes it out of its hole.
He dips a live turkey in bear grease.
He kills a deer and heads for home alone.
He throws enemies over a cliff; mutilates sole survivor.
Told to hunt "everything alive," he kills two men.
He lives alone, kills intruders, mutilates sole survivor.
Boy with thunderbird power becomes his partner.
He and his young partner meet giants.
Envious of the boy's power, W tries to kill him with an ax.
Boy takes revenge by chopping off W's headdress.
He decapitates the boy; the boy, restored, leaves him.
Death of the boy; W's marriage.
He holds up a tree, which pushes him into the ground.

*98. Story of Delawares and White People [Treaty with the Dutch, cf. Arrival of the Dutch]; Michelson, NAA 2776, f. 7; col. 1912; Okla.?; 1,600 words. The tribe was living on "Big River" when the whites came; the Delawares sent a party of warriors to another big river to investigate these Big Knives (*max̄aicī́ᵉkan*). Young Delawares incite war. The Delawares cannot kill a certain white warrior who is on the "waters," because a "big fish" (ship) deflects their shots. They make an effigy of him and kill it. Following the hostilities, many are dead on both sides. They make a treaty not to molest one another in the future.

99. [The Water Monster and the Sun]; Michelson, NAA 2776, f. 6; col. 1912; Okla.; Charles Elkhair; 1,700 words. A girl gives birth to a fish, which is thrown into a ditch. The ditch becomes a lake; the fish becomes enormous. The fish kills people who venture near the lake. Elders of the tribe offer a wampum reward to whomever can kill it. Two grandsons of a poor woman change to a raven and a pigeon, fly to the sun's house, obtain hot ashes, and return to the lake. One boy becomes a butterfly, flies close to the fish, and drops ashes, causing the lake to boil. Thus the fish is killed and the boys collect the reward.

*100. Otter Skin Dance [Origin of Otter Ceremony]; Michelson, NAA 2776, f. 8; col. 1912; Okla.?; 1,400 words. Parents release their child's pet otter when it has grown, tying a tobacco bag around its neck. Missing the pet, the child falls sick. A doctor determines that the otter is the cause. A ceremony is held; the child recovers. Extensive ceremonial details are given.

*101. When Munsees Went from Place to Place [Westward migration of the Munsees]; Michelson, NAA 2776, f. 13; Munsee text and trans.; col. 1912; Munsee of Kansas; 430 words. In New York the Munsees were friends of the Mohawks; the whites pushed them west to Pennsylvania, to Gnadenhütten, to an unnamed place during the (Revolutionary?) war, back to Gnadenhütten where a hundred were massacred, then to Canada, and finally to Kansas.

1928–1947

102. The Myth of Red Cedar and the Seven Stars [ORIGIN OF THE PLEIADES with TREE motif]; Speck, *Big House,* p. 171–73, Unami text and trans.; pub. 1931; E. Okla.; James C. Webber; 500 words. In the ancient time seven men disappeared. A group of "pure" youths found them as seven stones; people often went to visit these "prophets," but one day they vanished and reappeared as seven trees: pines and some cedars. Again they changed, this time into seven stars, the Pleiades. Details are given on the ritual and medicinal uses of cedar.

103. [ORIGIN OF THE PLEIADES with TREE motif]; Speck, *Big House,* p. 48; pub. 1931; E. Okla. "Seven meteors fell from the sky partly burying themselves in the ground. Some shamans soon discovered them and they disappeared. The shamans found them again in the form of seven pines trees. They used to consult with these pine trees. Finally they became transformed into the seven stars."

104. [Origin of Big House]; Speck, *Big House,* p. 80–85, Unami text and trans.; pub. 1931; E. Okla.; James C. Webber; 300 words (not counting ceremonial details). Long ago an earthquake made huge crevices, from which black fluid issued, and also dust and smoke said to be the breath of the Evil Spirit. Even animals were terrified. The Creator was angry. All the creatures held a council and planned the Big House and its rites. Extensive ceremonial details are given on p. 85ff. *Note:* Webber writes of interviewing an old woman who "touched upon the time the Delawares lived in Ohio, when the earthquick [*sic*] was exciting and relates how the black smoke streamed out of the great crevices in the ground and how white sand came out of these torences [torrents?] and how these sand deposits grew large wild Indian potatoes, and how the Lenapes use to go there and gather

quantities of them for years. The sand seem to be sort of a fertilizer to the wild potatoes in this case" (War Eagle, APS 932, p. 51).

105. Story of the Neglected Boy Whose Body Parts Turned into Quails; Montour, Munsee text and trans.; 1931; Six Nations; Josiah Montour; 100 words. A neglectful mother went off and left her little boy, who sang, "Pitiful, pitiful! / I am all alone. It seems like I shall turn into / a quail. *potc'pái!*" With each repetition of the song, one of his limbs, then his head, and finally his body fell down. Thus he became a flock of quail. Quail are that woman's son, and for this reason the Delaware do not like to kill them.

106. [LITERAL FOOL KILLS SLEEPING BABY, cf. Wehixamukes]; Montour; 1931; Six Nations; Josiah Montour; 200 words. Opening: "My story camps, called by name Jack." Jack was baby-sitting; they'd told him to kill any flies that bothered the baby. Flies landed on the baby's face. Jack picked up an ax and swatted the flies, thus killing the baby. Hoping to escape retribution, he killed a setting goose, covered himself with the feathers, and settled on the nest. When the people returned, he hissed at them (like a goose). They discovered him anyway, noticing his rear end sticking out. Jack was a small person, yet a man.

107. [Jack the builder, cf. Wehixamukes]; Montour; Six Nations; 1931; Josiah Montour. "Jack was building a bark house. As he was looking around he saw a piece of bark hanging down. Then he started to climb up on it. Then he cut it off. Then while on the bark he fell down. Hanging thus on the cut-off bark he crashed down." Cf. Nora Dean's story of Wehixamukes and the bark (149 and 155, below).

108. The Snow Born Child Legend [Snow Boy]; War Eagle, APS 930; written 1933; E. Okla.; James C. Webber; 380 words. A child born to a virgin had an unusually long penis. Other children angered him by poking it. He bit their fingers, turning the fingers black, as though frostbitten. At age seven or eight he departed on a stream, magically causing ice floes to cohere. He instructed people to give him an annual offering of hominy grits. In return he would show them the route of wounded game by the blood on his "body the snow." *Note:* Snow Boy dwells in the far north, did not become a star, and visits us in hunting season (War Eagle, APS 932, p. 9).

109. [Origin of Peyote]; Petrullo, pp. 34–36; pub. 1934; E. Okla.; James C. Webber; 800 words. After Comanches had raided Mexican Indians and

were fleeing, an exhausted Comanche woman lagged behind with her little boy. She stopped, but the boy went on, trying to catch up. Then he himself stopped and slept under a tree. The mother fell unconscious; saw a mysterious man who told her the boy would safely reach camp and told her to eat peyote and receive a new religion from the Creator; as the man sank into the earth, peyote appeared, and she ate of it. Then a man appeared who was "Peyote himself" and taught her the ceremonies.

110. [Origin of Peyote]; Petrullo, pp. 37–38; pub. 1934; E. Okla.; Joe Washington; 350 words. After a battle, one man found himself alone; he lay down, preparing to be killed by the enemy. Instead, the spirit of peyote came to him, told him that his children and other survivors of his tribe were safe, then said, "This is what I look like." The man saw peyote plants. The Peyote spoke to him, telling him of the ceremonies.

111. [Origin of Peyote]; Petrullo, pp. 38–40; pub. 1934; E. Okla.; Charles Elkhair; 450 words. After a hunting party, a young boy was missing. His sister went in search of him. Exhausted and thirsty, she lay down to die, facing west, her outstretched arms pointing north and south. She felt something cool in her left hand. A man appeared, assuring her that her brother was safe, then disappeared. The peyote in her left hand spoke to her, telling her how to use it.

112. [Origin of Peyote]; Petrullo, pp. 40–41; pub. 1934; Anadarko; 400 words. A Comanche girl seeks her brother, who has become lost while hunting. After two days she is exhausted and thirsty, hears a voice in the air, looks around, and finds peyote growing. She eats of it, feels good, and is assured by the voice that her brother is safe. She returns home and tells about the peyote.

113. [Origin of Big House]; Speck, *Oklahoma Delaware Ceremonies,* p. 18; col. 1928–32; pub. 1937; E. Okla.; Tom Half Moon; 250 words. An earthquake with black fluid revealed God's anger over the sins of the people. In a vision, certain "good" men learned of the Big House ceremony. (During the bursting forth of the black fluid, as from a volcano, women held their children to protect them. The innocent children cried out; this became the prayer cry of the Big House.)

114. [Origin of mask rite, cf. Origin of Big House]; Speck, *Oklahoma Delaware Ceremonies,* p. 19; col. 1928–32; pub. 1937; E. Okla.; Tom Half Moon

per pp. 17–18; 300 words. Formerly the Big House posts did not have carved faces. About the time the whites arrived, one man had a vision of a monster residing in the east, its body covered with hair, its face half red, half black. The visionary and another man traveled east and saw the monster, thus verifying its existence. To acquire its power they induced others to carve the faces and begin the Messingk rites associated with the Big House.

115. [Bear Pet]; Speck, *Oklahoma Delaware Ceremonies,* pp. 35–36, 41–42, Unami text and trans.; col. 1928–32 per p. 3; pub. 1937; E. Okla.; James C. Webber; 320 words. People had a bear as pet. When it was grown, a little girl fell sick, and the sweat doctor determined that there was a "sympathetic relation" between the bear and the child and that the bear was "spiritually pleading" with her. Thus the bear was given a gift of wampum and "liberated" with a prayer for its well-being. *Note:* The story is a charter for the Bear Ceremony.

116. [BEAR BOY]; Speck, *Oklahoma Delaware Ceremonies,* pp. 37–43, Unami text and trans.; col. 1928–32 per p. 3; pub. 1937; E. Okla.; James C. Webber; 650 words. A boy, while playing in the woods, disappeared. Later a young man hunting squirrels saw the boy and killed the boy's bear mother; he fetched the human boy and the bear cubs from their tree, brought them home, and made pets of the cubs. The boy then felt guilty because his bear mother had predicted the hunter's arrival and had told the boy to hold up his arrow (to signify the presence of a human so that there would be no shooting). When the cubs matured, the people hung wampum strings around their necks to protect them and sent them off, telling them to think of humans as their "relations." *Note:* The story is a charter for the Bear Ceremony (see pp. 30–34).

117. [Origin of corn dance, with motif OFFENDED CORN SPIRIT]; Speck, *Oklahoma Delaware Ceremonies,* pp. 86–87; col. 1928–32; pub. 1937; E. Okla.; James C. Webber; 600 words. Long ago the corn mother went away. People began to be hungry. A council of all the people determined that the corn mother was offended; it was decided to make two cornhusk masks with cornhusk leggings and conduct a corn harvest ceremony.

118. [Why the Munsee left Cattaraugus, motif: TRIBES SEPARATE OVER TRIVIAL INCIDENT]; Speck, *Celestial Bear,* p. 11; col. 1930s; Six Nations Munsee, "current in the band"; 250 words. While the Munsee were living

at Cattaraugus, a Seneca chief's daughter suffered a mysterious illness. A Delaware doctor cured the woman. But the Seneca grew suspicious that the Delaware doctor had caused the disease, since he was able to cure it so quickly. Learning that the Seneca planned to attack, the Delaware fled in the night. *Note:* Chief Joseph Montour adds the detail that the Delawares were warned by a pig (ibid., p. 12n). *Note:* According to William Fenton there are "a number of variants of how old Chief Cornplanter drove all of the Munsees out of the Conewango and Cattaraugus watersheds" (Fenton, "Review of *The Celestial Bear,*" p. 426).

119. [Origin of Big House]; Speck, *Celestial Bear,* pp. 41–42; col. 1930s; Six Nations Munsee; Chief Joseph Montour; 150 words. Miserable during a time of their waywardness, the people were traveling in a mountainous region in the "home country" (i.e., Delaware-Hudson territory) when they suddenly saw a stone face on a mountain. Impressed by this sign from the Creator, they carved the images of the Creator's face in wood and placed them in the Big House.

120. The Youths Transformed into Stars [ORIGIN OF PLEIADES]; Speck, *Celestial Bear,* p. 81; col. 1935; Six Nations Munsee; Nekatcit; 200 words. A shorter version of the story was later written down by Jesse Moses (see abstract 123). Here Nekatcit mentions that the island in question was in the Delaware River.

121. [BEAR BOY]; War Eagle, APS 932, pp. 60–64 and cf. p. 38; probably 1937 per p. 38; E. Okla.; James C. Webber; 780 words. A boy is reared by a bear who instructs him to avoid certain foods for purity's sake; thus the boy becomes invisible to hunters. This is the origin of childhood food taboos.

122. The Bear-Boy [BEAR BOY]; Speck, "The Boy-bear," reprinted in Speck's *Celestial Bear,* pp. 81–83; Six Nations Munsee; presumably narrated by Nekatcit, who died in 1938; 1,300 words. A man, his wife, and his parents made a journey "two sun-ups" north of the main camp. The two couples settled on either side of a marsh. The young wife, who had brought her baby, carried it across the marsh to visit the grandparents; on the way back a female bear took the baby from the mother. The husband returned to the main camp for help; the tribe's "twelve hunters" came and searched, but to no avail. At the "second bear-hunting time following the loss of the baby," hunters set out to get a bear for the bear feast. The bear

with her three cubs plus the bear boy were in a den. First a "lazy" hunter (whose eyes seemed closed) arrived, then a one-eyed hunter, then, on the third day, a wide-eyed hunter. Now the bears had to emerge. All were shot except the bear boy (as foretold by an old woman in camp who had dreamed the details of the bear hunt). The boy returned to his people, grew up, and led a bear hunt, but refused to participate in the capture of the bear or in the bear ceremony—because he had drunk bear's milk as a child and felt the bears were his brothers.

123. The Boys Who Ascended to the Sky [cf. ORIGIN OF THE PLEIADES]; Speck, *Celestial Bear,* pp. 79–81; 1939; Six Nations Munsee; written in 1939 by Jesse Moses after Nekatcit who died in 1938 (cf. 120, above); 900 words. To prepare twelve boys to become the future *luk-tha-weel-nu* (captains or principal men) of the tribe, a *luk-tha-weel-nu* took them to fast on an island and returned each day to test them, throwing each a corn cake that had to be caught on a sharpened stick (*Note:* The custom is described in Richard Adams, *Legends,* pp. 25–26). One by one the boys succeeded. But on the twelfth day, unbidden, they danced in a circle and rose to become a certain group of "small glittering stars in a circular formation with one at the center."

124. Story of Indian Summer [ORIGIN OF AUTUMN HAZE]; Moses, "Story of Indian Summer"; Six Nations; Jesse Moses. "Long ago, at the end of summer, after there had been the first frost, Man of the North and Man of the South got in dispute over who should rule the world. Man of the North said he would take control, and Man of the South said *he* would. Before they went further, they decided to hold council and sat down and smoked together. The smoke from their pipes rose and filled the air, and that is the haze of Indian summer."

125. *Wewtənúwe·s,* The Mermaid [The Water Monster and the Sun]; Voegelin, "Delaware Texts," pp. 105–6, Unami text and trans.; col. 1939; E. Okla.; Willie Longbone; 280 words. A young woman gave birth to a female child that was half fish and threw it into a lake. It grew large and began to kill children. Two young men went to the sun for fire, but the sun refused them, saying the heat would burn the whole earth. They went to the "night sun" (i.e., the moon), who gave them hot ashes. They threw the ashes into the lake where the monster lived; the lake boiled. Thus the "mermaid" was killed—but its many children remained wherever there was

water. *Note:* The teller adds a tradition about a scoffer who was plagued by the "mermaid" and thus suffered thirst.

126. *Mhú·we,* The Cannibal [WINTER CANNIBAL]; Voegelin, "Delaware Texts," pp. 106–10, Unami text and trans.; col. 1939; E. Okla.; Willie Longbone; 1,700 words. An episodic tale divided by Voegelin into 104 short sections:

(Secs. 1–11) Two disobedient women find a prostrate bird and pick it up, identifying it as "pure" (*pí·lsi·t*); they rub their genitals with the bird until it is dead. Its soul goes to heaven, where the False Face spirits live (cf. motif SPLIT BODY IN SKY WORLD), but the soul is too dirty to enter. One of the False Face spirits, taking pity on the soul, goes and tells people on earth that they have done wrong and must atone.

(Secs. 12–17) The people must sing for four days while their young women dance nude—but during the dance an old woman wraps a covering around one of the nude women (who is her granddaughter), thus invalidating the trial.

(Secs. 18–27) The spirit comes again and tells the people they must starve twelve babies until dead—but one of the mothers retrieves her child, thus again nullifying the trial.

(Secs. 28–32) Giving up on the project, the False Face advises the people to leave at midnight and seek refuge in a southern land. At dawn a killer snowfall covers the country they have left behind. Of the few who remain in the old country, one becomes a cannibal. Unable to find other food, he eats his fellows, then heads south to eat the refugees, who have been living well in the south, enjoying plenty of food.

(Secs. 33–46) A woman looking into her cooking pot sees the approaching cannibal reflected in the grease slick. She and her husband hide their baby. The cannibal arrives, smells the baby, and becomes hungry. His attention is diverted by a bag of grease, which he drinks; then he finds and eats some meat, then another bag of grease. Satisfied, he sleeps. When he wakes, the spell of cannibalism has left him because he has at last had "proper" food. A swarm of insects crawl out through his nose, signifying that the spell is broken.

(Secs. 47–52) The reformed cannibal warns his hosts that another cannibal from the old country will soon come and that he, the reformed cannibal, will fight the intruder, while the host and his wife must drive a stake into the intruder's anus. Thus the new cannibal arrives and is killed.

(Secs. 53–78) But now the reformed one, who has become their friend, warns the man and his wife that there are still many more cannibals—giants—in the north country and that the people must flee. Once again the refugees take flight, going to a farther country where they join other Delawares who are living there. In this farther country are two young men who decide to go north to see the cannibals. The little brother of one of the men tags along, becomes frightened, and has to be hidden under brush. The two men meet a giant, shoot him, drive a stake into his anus, and burn his body.

(Secs. 80–92) [PETITIONERS SELECT MAGICAL ATTRIBUTES with motif Would-be womanizer punished.] Each man takes a trophy. One takes a finger, with which he will be able to point at an enemy, thus weakening him. The other takes the giant's tongue, to put in his own mouth to whoop and terrorize enemies. The little brother takes an ear, so that "all women will make love to him."

(Secs. 93–103) Traveling home, they see women packing wood. Women rush the younger brother and fight over him, tearing off his limbs. Then the two men go to the chief, who asks them if they have done something. They tell him, "We did that for our younger brother: thus he begged for that and thus he got that."

(Sec. 104) Narrator concludes: "I break [it] off." *Note:* The narrator utters the final statement while breaking a stick across his knee (see "Willie's Tales," *Time,* Aug. 7, 1939, p. 45).

127. Wehixamukes, Crazy Jack; Voegelin, "Delaware Texts," pp. 110–13, Unami text and trans.; col. 1930; E. Okla.; Willie Longbone; 950 words. Episodic tale divided into 59 short sections:

(Secs. 1–20) A boy born with a finger missing (from each hand) grew fast, began to work miracles; he went out with hunters to get bear. The leader told all the men to "put their noses to the ground." The former boy, now trickster, took the instruction literally and buried his head in the ground with his buttocks sticking up.

(Secs. 21–39) Later, the trickster caught a bear and roasted it, as the grease dripped down and filled the holes around the roasting stakes. The men said they wished they had a turkey to dip in that grease. The trickster ran and caught a live turkey and started to dip it. The others ridiculed him, explaining to him that they meant roasted turkey meat.

(Secs. 40–46) Traveling on, the men see an enemy party and say to each other that they want to "throw them down on the ground." The trickster takes it literally and begins throwing the enemies to the ground. The others correct him and massacre the enemies. The trickster always says, "Flu! You should have told me straight."

(Secs. 47–59) Back home, the trickster meets his sisters-in-law, who are felling a tree. They tell him to catch it, since he is always boasting of his strength. He does, but its weight drives him halfway into the ground. Then he tells the women that he is departing this earth. At the world's end he will be reborn, again with one finger missing, will grow fast, and will fight magnificently in the war of the world's end, helping his fellows to "whip everybody."

128. When the Creator Was Drunk [DRUNKENNESS OF NOAH]; Voegelin, APS 4225b, Unami text and trans.; col. 1930s; E. Okla.; "LW" (probably should be WL, i.e., Willie Longbone); 60 words. When the Creator was drunk, a man who laughed at him turned black; another man, who pitied him, turned red; and a third was so scared he turned white.

129. [DANIEL IN THE LIONS' DEN]; War Eagle, APS 929; written 1939; E. Okla.; James C. Webber; 950 words. Two men are fast friends. But one of them, a witch, has a beautiful wife, whom he fears his friend covets. Thus he bewitches his friend, making him pregnant. Then he takes his friend on a hunting trip and pushes him over the brink of a pit filled with ferocious beasts (leopards, lions, etc.). Miraculously the beasts pity the man, cure his pregnancy, and allow him to return home. Back home, the man tells all. The beasts come and suck out the witch's insides.

130. Deserted boy and his dog; War Eagle, APS 932, pp. 85–87; written 1939; E. Okla.; James C. Webber; 470 words. A deserted boy finds a puppy and cares for it; it brings him hunting power and the power to find his tribe. People envy him, women want him. Enemies kill his dog; he loses his hunting power and becomes pitiful. The dog was his *we,tse* (friend, spiritual helper).

131. [BEAR BOY]; Tantaquidgeon, p. 68; pub. 1942; E. Okla.; James C. Webber. Very close variant, almost a repeat, of 116, above.

132. The Woods Dwarf [Wemategunis]; Tantaquidgeon, pp. 68–69; pub. 1942; E. Okla.; James C. Webber: 180 words. While playing alone in the forest a little boy met *Maté·kanis,* a brown creature resembling a small boy but strong and powerful. *Maté·kanis* is kind, always helping people, but

he is rarely seen. The boy went often to play with the dwarf. Sometimes, while with other children, he would catch sight of the dwarf and point to him, but the others could not see him. Nowadays the people never see these dwarfs because the Delawares have adopted modern ways and are thus no longer "clean enough."

133. [Wemategunis]; War Eagle, APS 931; 1943; E. Okla.; James C. Webber; 200 words. Matekanes was a little dwarf who lived in the woods and had more power than Mesingkalikan. A man who had this spirit as his guardian offended it by boasting of his hunting ability. Thus he lost his hunting power. It is said that the dwarf herds game so that people cannot find it, rides on the back of a deer, and carries a bow and arrows.

134. The Seven Wise Men [ORIGIN OF THE PLEIADES]; Tantaquidgeon, p. 69; pub. 1942; E. Okla.; James C. Webber. Very close variant, almost a repeat of 103, above—but here the trees are all cedars; pine is not mentioned.

135. [The three races, cf. ORIGIN OF THE THREE RACES]; War Eagle, APS 932, p. 24; 1943; E. Okla.; James C. Webber. "I picked up a story pertaning to the races, in detail, as it is related, it was a fire burning. Denoteation human beings. The red blazes denote red man & ashes the white man antispated & the black coals denote the presence of a black race. Very interesting. Yours, War Eagle."

136. [The earthquake and the dove, cf. biblical DELUGE]; Gilliland, True Religion, p. 17; received by the Smithsonian in 1947; E. Okla.; Gilliland; 130 words. Long ago the earth trembled for three moons; thinking God was angry, the people prayed in their "church house." They could hardly cook, because as the earth shook, their fires would go out. One morning at sunrise a turtledove perched on a little tree and cooed, and the earth "settled down." Thus the turtledove is sacred, never killed.

137. [TOWER OF BABEL]; Gilliland, True Religion, p. 18; received by the Smithsonian in 1947; E. Okla.; Gilliland; 140 words. Long ago the Indians all spoke the same language. They began building a tower of stone to heaven, but God gave them different languages one night as they slept. They had to stop working together on the building because they could no longer understand each other. Thus the tribes in the United States have many different languages.

138. The Corn Legend; Gilliland, True Religion, pp. 18A–19; received by the Smithsonian in 1947; E. Okla.; Gilliland; 130 words. A youth refuses to hunt because the animals are his friends. Disgusted, his father, the chief, drives him from camp. Winter comes. The boy is about to starve. Then he sees a "large light." It is the "Great father Jesus," telling him to go to a certain stump (where he will find corn to eat?) but to leave seed for planting. Next year, after his corn has been harvested, he returns to camp and becomes a hero. From then on the people have corn—a hollowed-out stump is used as the mortar.

1950–1992

139. [The boy who hoped for rain; cf. Thunder's Helper]; Newcomb, p. 73; pub. 1956; E. Okla.; Fred Washington; 240 words. An old woman berated her little grandson for being worthless. There was a drought. The boy went off and hoped for rain four times. Thunder and rain came. The boy departed saying, "When you hear the lightning cracking around . . . it's me." People say the cracking of thunder is the boy; the heavy rumbling is the old thunderbirds. Motif: VOICE OF YOUNG THUNDER.

140. [Man Who Visited the Thunders]; Newcomb, pp. 73–74; pub. 1956; E. Okla.; Jim Thompson; 110 words. A man says he will go live with the Thunders; people doubt him because he has no wings. But he builds a fire on top of a huge rock, and when it is "almost red hot" he pushes it over the cliff into the river. As steam rises, he jumps into it and disappears. Later he returns from the sky.

141. [THE HUNTERS AND THE WATER MONSTER]; Newcomb, p. 74; pub. 1956; E. Okla.; Jim Thompson; 220 words. A hunter follows a turkey call coming from a lake, but it is a water monster. The monster drowns him and eats him. Two or three others are also caught by this "snake." Several boys who are ritually "clean" go to the sun for advice. Sun tells them to gather sweepings from the west end of the Big House and sprinkle these around the lake. They do so, the lake boils, and the monster dies.

142. [Thunder's Helper]; Newcomb, p. 74; pub. 1956; E. Okla.; Martha Bob; 460 words. A certain boy is different, won't hunt. In order to "take care of him," his grandfather leads him to an island, abandons him, and prays for him, using tobacco to "make the boy wise." Alone, the boy is frantic; he cries. On the fifth day he hears the voice of a skunk, offering

to take him home; but another voice warns that the skunk is too small to be the boy's helper. Next day a horned serpent offers to take the boy home but tells him to sound a warning if a dark cloud appears. Halfway to shore, the boy gives the warning and the serpent turns back. Next day they try again. This time the boy omits the warning. They reach the shore, where the seven Thunders kill the serpent and eat it. The grandfather now instructs the boy to kill a bear, thus supplying a feast. After that, the boy is just like other boys.

143. [Girl sacrificed to horned serpent, cf. SERPENT'S BRIDE]; Newcomb, p. 75, paraphrase only; pub. 1956; E. Okla.; Martha Bob. All the youths love one girl, but adults will not permit marriage. Instead the girl is married off to the Horned Serpent, who then plagues the people no more.

144. [LOSS OF THE ANCIENTS with motifs STUPID GIANT and WINTER CANNIBAL]; Newcomb, p. 75; pub. 1956; E. Okla.; Fred Washington; 220 words. Women gathering firewood offend an eagle by capturing it. It escapes and reports to the Powers, who punish the offense by sending snow for ten days, which buries the houses. Unable to get food, people become cannibals; they grow until they are giants. It is they who are buried in the Indian mounds. One day a family saw one of these giants and fled across a creek. The giant approached the creek with its walking staff; it measured the water's depth horizontally instead of vertically and thus stupidly thought the (shallow) stream was too deep to cross. The family escaped.

145. [Rising Star Children Hit by Clothes, cf. ORIGIN OF THE PLEIADES]; Newcomb, p. 75; pub. 1956; E. Okla.; Jim Thompson; 60 words. During a recess in the Big House ceremony, seven boys began to rise; people threw unclean clothing at them and knocked two of them back down. The others became "those stars."

146. [Origin of Doll Dance]; Newcomb, p. 76; pub. 1956; E. Okla.; Jim Thompson; 140 words. A girl who loved to play with dolls was told in a dream to make a certain doll and give it feasts because dolls take care of crops. She awoke, went to the woods, and carved the doll she had seen in her dream.

147. [Punishment for unauthorized doll dance]; Newcomb, p. 76; pub. 1956; E. Okla.; Jim Thompson; 110 words. While their parents were away at a Doll Dance, children decided to stage their own version of the cere-

mony. This dangerous act caused one child to become sick. The child was cured by a regular Doll Dance.

148. [Mother-in-Law Story]; Newcomb, p. 76; pub. 1956; E. Okla.; Jim Thompson and Martha Bob; 180 words. A man tricks his disagreeable mother-in-law by jiggling lily pads and calling out, "Your son-in-law is going to die." She weeps. Later, seeing that he is alive after all, she reforms and treats him well.

149. One Story About Wehixamukes [Wehixamukes]; Rementer, ed., Christmas letters, Unami text and trans.; col. 1968; E. Okla.; Nora Dean; 200 words. Wehixamukes wounds himself with an ax; climbs a tree to apply healing bark.

150. Here Again Is a Wehixamukes Story [Wehixamukes]; Rementer, ed., Christmas letters, Unami text and trans.; col. 1968; E. Okla.; Nora Dean; 200 words. W dips the turkey in grease (see 79, 97, and 127, above; and 155, below).

151. The Stubborn Girl [The Dog Who Wanted to Warm Himself]; Pearson, *Grammar*, pp. 197–219; Unami text and trans.; col. 1968–71; E. Okla.; Nora Dean; 270 words. When the Delawares still lived in the east, a strange dog was annoyed by a girl who kept preventing him from lying by the fire, asking him to tell a story. Finally the dog said to her, "Three days from now you will be under the red dirt," and in three days she was dead. From this comes the admonition not to question or abuse dogs. Moreover, dogs must be treated with respect because they guard the bridge to the afterworld, the bridge that lies at the fork in the Milky Way (motif: DOG GUARDS ROUTE TO AFTERWORLD).

152. [GOOD AND EVIL CREATORS]; Kraft, 163; col. 1969; E. Okla.; Nora Dean. Kishelëmukòng made useful plants, Mahtantu made poisonous ones; K made edible berries, M put thorns on the bushes; M made noxious insects and snakes.

153. The Man and His Dog; Rementer, ed., Christmas letters, Unami text and trans. (pub. 1985 in Kraft and Kraft, p. 41); E. Okla.; Nora Dean; 220 words. A dog, to oblige its master, killed a snake and thereafter demanded to be fed at the table.

154. The Origin of the Bittersweet Vine; Rementer, ed., Christmas letters, Unami text and trans.; E. Okla.; Nora Dean; 200 words. A jealous owl slapped his wife, knocking off her red earring. From this grew the bittersweet vine.

155. Wehixamukes Story; Pearson, Notebook, pp. 12–19; Unami text and trans.; E. Okla.; Nora Dean; 550 words. Wehixamukes acts foolish but is powerful and wise. Told to heal his ax wound with a bark application, he climbs a tree. Hearing that the head man wants to eat turkey dipped in grease, he dips a live turkey in a kettle of grease. Another time he alerts an enemy war party by crying, "Here we are!" He redeems himself, however, by killing them all.

156. More Wehixamukes; Pearson, Notebook, pp. 21–33; Unami text and trans.; E. Okla; Nora Dean; 750 words. Back east in Pennsylvania the Delawares went hunting and took Wehixamukes with them. Knowing that enemies were near, Wehixamukes decoyed them by covering his head with a deer's bladder as if he had been scalped. Thus he killed them all. His companions now believed he was powerful. At last he announced that his time to die had come. But he said he would return as a boy with one finger missing; he would be born to a virgin, he said, at a time when the whites would have become intolerably oppressive. Next day a felled tree drove him into the ground. All mourned his loss.

157. The Origin of the Big House [Rising Star Children Hit by Clothes]; Pearson, Notebook, pp. 37–48; Unami text and trans.: E. Okla.; Nora Dean; 750 words. Back east in New Jersey and Pennsylvania the whites broke their treaty with the Nanticokes and the Delawares, forcing these tribes to migrate westward. At White River, Indiana, the Delawares burned an old Nanticoke woman as a witch; other people were also burned as witches. Angry, the Creator sent an earthquake and a windstorm. People wished to appease the Creator. In a vision, one old man saw a bear-robed spirit with a turtle rattle. Also, the people summoned children to make prayers, since children are "pure." As the children began rising to the sky, the people tried to bring them back to earth by pelting them with soiled menstrual clothes. Seven girls, unhit, rose to become the Pleiades, which are now seen in autumn. This was the beginning of the Big House ceremonies.

158. The Foolish Man; Pearson, Notebook, pp. 83–87; Unami text and trans.; E. Okla.; Nora Dean; 220 words. A man who boasted of his attractiveness, and who liked to be fondled by women, played a frequent trick: he pulled valuable rings from his pocket and threatened to burn them. Thus tantalized, women would fondle him, begging him for the rings. Eventually everyone hated this man.

159. Pepper Bottle [WHY DOGS SNIFF ONE ANOTHER]; Pearson, Notebook, pp. 89–99; Unami text and trans.; E. Okla.; Nora Dean; 350 words. Essentially the same as 168 and 179, below.

160. Mermaid Story [The Water Monster and the Sun]; Pearson, Notebook, pp. 113–25; Unami text and trans.; E. Okla.; Nora Dean; 380 words. A stubborn girl disobeyed the injunction not to bathe nude, and a spirit impregnated her. She gave birth to a monster, half human, half fish. She threw it into the lake. Later, children who bathed there were drowned, presumably by the monster. Two boys volunteered to kill it, traveled to the sun on sunbeams, obtained hot ashes, and threw these into the lake. Thus the water boiled, killing the monster. The Shawnee and other tribes took pieces of the corpse and thereafter used them in their ceremonial dances.

161. Three Boys on a Vision Quest [PETITIONERS SELECT MAGICAL ATTRIBUTES with motif Would-be womanizer punished]; Rementer, Letters on Delaware Folklore, 11 May 1990; E. Okla.; Warren Longbone; 130 words. Three boys on a vision quest meet a manito (manitou) who grants each his wish: war medicine, hunting luck, and success with women. The boy who made the last of these wishes is attacked and killed by amorous women.

162. The Giant Squirrel Story; Rementer, Letters on Delaware Folklore, 11 May 1990 (trans. only); Unami text and trans. in Rementer, ed., Christmas letters; col. 1975; E. Okla.; Nora Dean; 250 words. The giant man-eating squirrel of ancient time is reduced by the Creator, who leaves a handprint under the squirrel's arm as a mark of shame.

163. Origin of the Delaware Woman Dance [ORPHEUS]; Rementer, Letters on Delaware Folklore, 11 May 1990; col. 1979; Okla.; Lillie Whitehorn; 800 words. A man went off to shoot turkeys; while he was gone, his wife was struck dead by Thunders (cf. THE HUNTERS AND THE WATER

MONSTER). In council, another man offered to bring the victim back from the dead if the women would dance, if the victim's son was withheld from her, and if no one cried. The woman did return; but one old man cried, and she disappeared.

164. [Man Who Visited the Thunders]; Dean, "Reminiscences," p. 5; col. 1975; pub. 1978; E. Okla.; Nora Dean; 220 words. A man builds a fire to heat a huge rock. He pushes the rock over the edge of a cliff into the river. As steam rises, he rises with it to where the Thunders live. He discovers that the Thunders eat bone soup. They tell him the sharp thunder is the voice of young Thunders (motif: VOICE OF YOUNG THUNDER); deep rumbling is the voice of the old Thunders. After a few days the man jumps on a low cloud and returns to earth.

165. The Fox and the Rabbit; Dean, "Reminiscences," p. 10; col. 1975; pub. 1978; E. Okla.; Nora Dean; 440 words. An industrious Fox sees that his garden is ravaged. He plants sharp stakes and the next day finds blood and rabbit fur on them. He then goes to visit Rabbit, who is sick in bed with his wounds. Rabbit pretends innocence. The angry Fox punches him in the face. Moral: Do not lie, because you will be found out sooner or later.

166. The Dog Who Wanted to Warm Himself; Dean, "Reminiscences," pp. 10–11; col. 1975; pub. 1978; E. Okla.; Nora Dean; 300 words. Much the same as 151, above, but with this "moral": Never ask dogs questions; they might tell you something you don't want to hear.

167. You Should Have Told Me So! [Wehixamukes]; Dean, "Reminiscences," p. 11; col. 1975; pub. 1978; Nora Dean; 300 words. Wehixamúkes was actually very wise, only seemed silly. He tended camp while the other men hunted. One day he hurt his hand. They told him to tie bark on it. When they returned, they found him high in a tree with his hand tied to the bark. When they scolded him, he said, "You should have told me." Another time Wehixamúkes heard some of the hunters, while eating, say that they wished they had a turkey to dip in the grease. Next day he caught a turkey, and when they returned, they found him dipping the whole bird, feathers and all, in grease. As usual, he protested, "You should have told me."

168. The Dogs Are Looking for Something! [WHY DOGS SNIFF EACH OTHER]; Dean, "Reminiscences," pp. 11–12; col. 1975; pub. 1978; E. Okla.;

Nora Dean; 550 words. "You know, you see dogs, they smell each other when they meet. Well, they're looking for something!" It seems that dogs and coyotes used to live together. But one dog went off to bring back fire and stayed with humans as a pet. The coyotes were angry, accusing the dogs of deceit. Thus the dogs and the coyotes separated. After that, dogs had their own council meetings. To show how pure and holy they were, they had a rule that all had to deposit their *kekunëmëwo* in a basket at the door. One day a wolf came to the door, scaring them so that they all fled in haste, each grabbing one of the *kekunëmëwo* (genitals; literally, "your things"). Since most got the wrong one, they are still searching to this day (thus sniffing each other when they meet).

169. The Trickster [Wehixamukes]; Dean, "Reminiscences," p. 12; col. 1975; pub. 1978; E. Okla.; Nora Dean; 240 words. While lying in ambush with a war party, Wehixamúkes foolishly jumped up and said, "here we are, here we are." As punishment, his comrades made him go alone to kill the enemy. So he shot a deer, put its bloody bladder on his head as if he had been scalped, and lay down on the trail. Enemies came along and thought he was dead; he jumped up, killed them all, and returned to tell his fellows.

170. [Story about Wewtunëwes, the merman: The Water Monster and the Sun]; Dean, "Reminiscences," pp. 12–13; col. 1975; pub. 1978; E. Okla.; Nora Dean; 480 words. Wewtunëwes drew children under the water and drowned them as they swam in the lake. Boys climbed *wipeko* ("shadows," i.e., sunbeams) to the sky and obtained hot dust from the sun. With this they made the lake boil, and the monster was killed. Each tribe, including the Shawnee, got a piece of him. The Delaware's piece is in the Museum of the American Indian (in New York). *Note:* For illustrations of Delaware medicine bundles containing mica flakes (regarded as serpent scales), see Harrington, "Some Customs," p. 54; "Sketch," pp. 225–26.

171. [Rising Star Children Hit by Clothes, cf. ORIGIN OF PLEIADES]; Dean, "Reminiscences," p. 15; col. 1975; pub. 1978; E. Okla.; Nora Dean; 230 words. The Big House was instituted during an earthquake, sent as punishment for the burning of innocent people as witches at White River, Indiana. Little boys were lined up and told to pray to the Creator, because these boys were "clean." As they prayed, they rose into the air. People threw old clothing at them; some fell back to earth. Those that ascended became the seven stars, the Pleiades.

172. Clan Bragging Story [Turtle Phratry Is Best]; Andrew Twaddle quoted in Rementer, "Humor," p. 3; col. 1975; E. Okla.; Nora Dean; 170 words. A Wolf Clan woman sees a dog carrying a turtle and brags that her clan is stronger; Turtle Clan woman says this only shows that the Turtle Clan is smarter, because the turtle is getting the ride.

173. Why the Rabbit Looks the Way He Does; Rementer, "Humor"; col. 1977; W. Okla.; Martha Ellis. Close variant of 210, below.

174. [BEAR BOY]; Dean, Place names, tape 16, side A, count 188–207; col. 1976; E. Okla.; Nora Dean; 160 words. A boy lost in the woods was adopted by a mother bear, who nursed him and brought him up. Hunters came and shot the bear mother; took the boy back to camp and "tamed" him.

175. The Stubborn Girl [The Dog Who Wanted to Warm Himself]; Dean, Place names, tape 16, side A, count 414–75; col. 1976; E. Okla.; Nora Dean. Virtually the same as 151 and 166, above.

176. The Stubborn Girl; Dean, Stories in Lenape and English, tape 52a, side A, count 59–107, Unami text and English paraphrase; col. 1977; E. Okla.; Nora Dean. Virtually the same as 175, above.

177. [The Fox and the Rabbit]; Dean, Stories in Lenape and English, tape 52a, side A, count 138–205, Unami text and English paraphrase; col. 1977; E. Okla.; Nora Dean; 350 words. Similar to 165, above.

178. [Man Who Visited the Thunders]; Dean, Stories in Lenape and English, tape 52A, side A, count 208–86, Unami text and English paraphrase, text transcribed with literal English trans. in Rementer, ed., Christmas letters; col. 1977; E. Okla.; Nora Dean; 250 words. Similar to 164, above.

179. [WHY DOGS SNIFF ONE ANOTHER]; Dean, Stories in Lenape and English, tape 52a, side A, count 344–73; col. 1977; E. Okla.; Nora Dean; 300 words. Similar to 168, above.

180. [WHITE MAN CREATED FROM FOAM]; Dean, Stories in Lenape and English, tape 52a, side B, count 180–205, Unami text and English paraphrase; col. 1977; E. Okla.; Nora Dean; 50 words. The ocean beat against a rock on the shore until the foam formed a person.

181. [The Giant Squirrel Story]; Dean, Stories in Lenape and English, tape 52a, side B, count 207–76, Unami text and English paraphrase; col. 1977; E. Okla.; Nora Dean. Much the same as 162, above, but with this final comment: "I've dressed many squirrels, and there's a little hand right here, and we was told not to ever eat that, so I always cut it out."

182. [The Water Monster and the Sun]; Dean, Stories in Lenape and English, tape 52a, side B, count 405–38, Unami text and English paraphrase; col. 1977; E. Okla.; Nora Dean. Much the same as 170, above, but with the opening "This is a story about [when] the Lenape people were in the east."

183. [DRUNKENNESS OF NOAH]; Dean, Delaware beliefs, tape 53b, side A, count 15–34; col. 1977; E. Okla.; Nora Dean; 180 words. In order to learn what humans felt about him, the Creator pretended to be "real bad sick" (drunkenness is not mentioned). The white man waited on him hand and foot; the black man laughed at him; the Indian just stood back in silence. Thus the Creator blessed the whites and punished the others.

184. [Arrival of the Whites, cf. Arrival of the Dutch]; Dean, Delaware beliefs, tape 53b, side A, count 64–83; col. 1977; E. Okla.; 180 words; Nora Dean. A Delaware predicted the arrival of the whites. When the whites came, the Delawares spread furs for them to walk on.

185. [Rising Star Children Hit by Clothes, cf. ORIGIN OF PLEIADES]; Dean, Delaware beliefs, tape 53b, side B, count 125–45; col. 1977; E. Okla.; Nora Dean. Essentially as in 167, above, but with the added information that one of Nora Dean's "aunts" was burned as a witch when the people were in Indiana.

186. Snake Story; Aikens, Family, side B; col. 1977; told in English; told "in the [Munsee] Delaware" in Aikens, Snake story, side A; Morpeth, Ontario; Hannah Aikens (who calls it an "eastern" story); 450 words. A white serpent (representing European Americans) battled a black serpent (African Americans), until the two joined forces when confronted by a red serpent (Communists). The Indians stayed out of it.

187. [Turtle as EARTH DIVER]; Aikens, Snake story, side A, count 356–71; col. 1977; Morpeth, Ontario; Hannah Aikens (who calls it an "eastern" story); 100 words. The turtle is "the mother of the earth" because in the beginning it dived into the water and came up with mud that the Great

Spirit used to form land. Thus the turtle is the "symbol of the world" (cf. TURTLE ISLAND).

188. [Turtle discovers the earth is round]; Aikens, Snake story, side A, count 372–425; col. 1977; Morpeth, Ontario; Hannah Aikens (who calls it an "eastern" story); 350 words. In the beginning the animals could talk to one another. They decided to find out how far one would have to go before "falling off" into the water. Fox went but fooled around and came back; bear went but fell asleep in a cave. Turtle went and traveled under the ocean and around the world, returning home. This is how it was discovered that the earth is round—and why the turtle is persistent.

189. [Mother-in-Law Story]; Robt. Adams, *Music,* p. 124 (with song transcribed on p. 166); col. before 1977; E. Okla.; Nora Dean; 120 words. A man whose mother-in-law hates him hides near the lake when she comes for water. Using a string tied to lily pads, he shakes the pads and sings, "They will die, a person, if she hates her son-in-law." Thus warned, she meets the son-in-law later and tells him, "I love you."

190. [Squirrel defies boy hunter]; Robt. Adams, *Music,* p. 125 (with song transcribed on p. 166); col. before 1977; E. Okla.; Nora Dean; 120 words. A squirrel "ran inside of a tree" to escape a boy hunter, who then put rocks all around the tree to lock up the squirrel. Next morning the boy returned and heard the squirrel singing, "Never will you starve me to death, little boy, little boy." Frightened, the boy ran home and repeated the song for his parents.

191. Dinosaur Story [THE HUNTERS AND THE WATER MONSTER]; Hale, *Cooley's,* p. 5, Unami text and trans.; col. 1977–80; W. Okla.; Bessie Snake; 420 words. Twelve men went hunting with a dog. A dinosaur ate all but the twelfth, a boy, who told the dog to throw ashes from the campfire into the beast's mouth. This killed it, burning it up. Later the ashes were used as a love charm.

192. The Hunter Who Had But One Bullet [FORTUNATE HUNTER]; Hale, *Cooley's,* p. 26, Unami text and trans.; col. 1977–80; W. Okla.; Martha Ellis; 350 words. A man who has only one arrow and one bullet goes hunting; ties ducks. They lift him into the sky (motif: FORTUNATE HUNTER FLIES WITH GEESE); he jumps down and splashes a big catfish onto the bank; cuts it open and finds a baby bear.

193. The Hummingbird and the Turtle [TURTLE WINS RACE]; Hale, *Cooley's,* p. 44, Unami text and trans.; col. 1977–80; W. Okla.; Willie Snake; 180 words. Turtle wins by tricking hummingbird: he substitutes another turtle at the finish line.

194. Foot Log to Heaven [DOG GUARDS ROUTE TO AFTERWORLD]; Hale, *Cooley's,* p. 50, Unami text and trans.; col. 1977–80; W. Okla.; Bessie Snake; 120 words. Dogs guard the log bridge to heaven, toppling souls into the water if they have mistreated dogs on earth.

195. [The Water Monster and the Sun]; Howard, p. 190; pub. 1981; E. Okla.; Nora Dean; 210 words. Giant Horned Snake causes many to drown in a lake. Two pure young men climb sunbeams to reach Our Brother the Sun, return with hot solar ashes, and put them into the lake. The lake boils, killing the serpent. Two shamans finish it off and divide its flesh among the tribes. Thus Delawares and others (including Shawnees) receive pieces of the flesh for their sacred bundles (Delaware bundle is in the American Museum of Natural History).

196. The Wolves and Dogs Fear Each Other; Rementer, ed., Christmas letters, Unami text and trans.; col. 1983; E. Okla.; Nora Dean; 190 words. In the ancient time the wolves sent a dog to steal fire; it became a pet and never returned.

197. [Man Who Visited the Thunders]; Brawer, *Many Trails,* p. 36; pub. 1983; E. Okla.; Nora Dean. "There is a story about a powerful Lenape man who visited and ate with the Pethakhuweyok (Thunder Beings). He said they make a rich soup from old, dry bones. After he visited these Thunderers for a while, he returned to the earth by jumping from a low-hanging cloud."

198. Delaware Crossing the Ice [MIGRATION ACROSS OCEAN]; Hale, *Turtle Tales,* p. 5; col. 1983–84; W. Okla.; Martha Ellis; 100 words. "My mother" used to say we came from another island and crossed the ice near the North Pole.

199. The Altar to Heaven [TOWER OF BABEL]; Hale, *Turtle Tales,* p. 5; col. 1983–84; W. Okla.; Willard Thomas; 90 words. All people spoke one language. While building a high altar to reach heaven, they fell to arguing and their voices changed.

200. The Man Who Went to Heaven After His Wife [MOTHER OF GHOSTS]; Hale, *Turtle Tales,* pp. 5–6; col. 1983–84; W. Okla.; Bessie Snake; 600 words. A wife disappears while fetching water, evidently abducted by a "man in the water" (called a "mermaid"), who has taken her to heaven. Her husband searches for her. When he reaches Heaven, which is guarded by an old woman called "grandmother," the old woman hides him from the ghosts who live there and gives him a gourd flask (to capture his wife's soul?). He then comes back to earth and dances with his fellow mortals to restore the dead wife. After dancing four times he shuts the gourd (to capture the soul?), and his wife appears in the flesh. But at that moment an old man cries, thus breaking an admonition not to weep. With that the wife disappears and returns to heaven.

201. Old Woman Who Was Weaving [ETERNAL WEAVER]; Hale, *Turtle Tales,* pp. 6–7; col. 1983–84; W. Okla.; Martha Ellis; 130 words. An old woman who owns one kernel of corn (INEXHAUSTIBLE FOOD SUPPLY) weaves a basket that mice chew at night (thus unraveling it?). If she were ever to finish the basket, the world would end.

202. The Horned Snake Legend [SERPENT'S BRIDE]; Hale, *Turtle Tales,* pp. 7–8; col. 1983–84; W. Okla.; Martha Ellis; 1,000 words. A young woman returning from her menstrual seclusion met a handsome youth who took her to his rock-den home. His mother was living there with him. Every day the young man would go out hunting. But he evidently feared thunder. The bride, having become uneasy, took flight, joined by her mother-in-law. A horned serpent started to pursue the two but fell dead on the shore of the river. Twelve women appeared and informed the bride they had killed and eaten the serpent (motif: Twelve women). Returning to her people, the young woman was met by "a little boy with a big stomach" (cf. Wemategunis?), who punctured her abdomen with arrows, thus removing her snake children. She hadn't realized she had been living underwater with the horned serpent.

203. Flag Story [Arrival of the Dutch]; Hale, *Turtle Tales,* p. 9; col. 1983–84; W. Okla.; Martha Ellis; 580 words. A youth predicts the arrival of a visitor with red hair and gray eyes; people spread otter fur at the seashore; a ship arrives, but the visitor refuses to step on the fur because he thinks it is too beautiful. The visitor presents an ax and a hoe, which the chief then wears around his neck. The whites trick the Delawares in a land sale, using string cut from a hide (cf. DIDO'S PURCHASE OF CARTHAGE). Whites and

Delawares fight. Tecumseh joins the fray. After the conflict, bones of the slain are buried; crossed chains over the grave signify peace. A Delaware man originates the United States flag.

204. Mamuui—The Eater [STONE GIANT]; Hale, *Turtle Tales,* p. 10; col. 1983–84; W. Okla; Bessie Hunter; 130 words. A man rolls in tar and gravel repeatedly, thus coating himself with an armor that makes him invulnerable to arrows. Thereafter he eats people with impunity. *Note:* Stories like this were told to make children behave (ibid., p. 36).

205. Boy Who Couldn't Hunt; Hale, *Turtle Tales,* p. 10; col. 1983–84; W. Okla.; Winnie Chisholm Poolaw; 270 words. A boy's grandmother admonishes him to be a hunter. When his sister kills a bird, the boy takes credit, deceiving the blind old grandmother.

206. Deer and the Peach Tree; Hale, *Turtle Tales,* p. 10; col. 1983–84; W. Okla.; Winnie Chisholm Poolaw; 130 words. A man shoots a deer, using an arrow tipped with a peach pit. A peach tree grows from the deer.

207. Doll Story; Hale, *Turtle Tales,* p. 11; col. 1983–84; W. Okla.; Martha Ellis; 360 words. An old woman had a doll that she fed ritually each summer; then the people could eat. The doll was handed down to a younger woman who tried unsuccessfully to get rid of it; it kept coming back. A boy tried to throw it away and became insane. Cf. Origin of Doll Dance.

208. Screech Owl Story; Hale, *Turtle Tales,* p. 12; col. 1983–84; W. Okla.; Winnie Poolaw and Martha Ellis; 140 words. When an owl comes indoors, a boy kills it, knowing it is a witch.

209. Witch Story; Hale, *Turtle Tales,* p. 12; col. 1983–84; W. Okla.; Winnie Poolaw; 290 words. A girl took sick. At night her mother saw a monster, half dog, half man, near the girl's bed. She hit it with a corn pounder. Next day she learned that an "old lady" had died in the night when a log fell on her.

210. Rabbit Story; Hale, *Turtle Tales,* pp. 14–15; col. 1983–84; W. Okla.; Martha Ellis; 180 words. Rabbit explains to the other animals that he has the ability to hide because, simply enough, it is easy for him to do so. He has long ears, he says, because he was once a messenger and needed to hear all the messages he was charged to deliver. He has a split lip from sitting

in council where he would always be asked "to fix the pipe so they could smoke it." Finally, he has narrow shoulders because he once had two wives: he always slept in the middle, and his wives squeezed him while he slept.

211. Icicle Baby [Snow Boy]; paraphrased in Rementer, Letters on Delaware Folklore, 25 April 1990; col. by Nora Dean. Rementer writes: "Told by a woman of Munsee descent, but she spoke Lenape better than Munsee. The gist of it is that a woman became pregnant by eating an icicle. When she had her baby, everyone who touched it became frozen. They tried putting ashes on it, to no avail, so it was taken to the creek and set afloat. Now, if anyone wants to cross a creek [in winter only?], they must throw some coarse cornmeal on the water or ice."

212. Three Rock Sisters; paraphrased in Rementer, Letters on Delaware Folklore, 25 April 1990. Rementer writes: "Told by an old woman . . . a very confusing story. The gist of it is that there were once three sisters who used to go up on a hill. One of them had a child, and she went to the hill and never returned. A rock shaped like her holding a baby was found on the hill later. . . ."

213. [ORIGIN OF THE THREE RACES]; Rementer, Letters on Delaware Folklore, 5 July 1990. Rementer writes: "One story I have heard, although I heard versions of this from several tribes, is the one about the Creator forming a human and baking it. The first one was underdone and very pale, and he threw it down saying that it wasn't quite right. This became the white race. The next one he baked too long, and it was very dark. He threw it down, and it was the black race. The third one he baked came out just right, and he was well pleased with it. That was the Indian."

214. Mother-in-Law Story; Ellis, included with Rementer, Letters on Delaware Folklore, 4 Sept. 1990; Unami text and trans.; W. Okla.; Martha Ellis; 680 words. A man is disconsolate because his mother-in-law hates him. At the lakeside a stranger in yellow and green advises the man to trick his mother-in-law when she comes for water. Thus the man takes strips of elm bark, ties these to cattails, (and jiggles them?—as in 148, above), calling out a threat of death to any woman who hates her son-in-law. Terrified, the woman treats her son-in-law lovingly thereafter, and softens his hide clothing for him. The helpful stranger is revealed as a bullfrog.

215. Cutting the Hide Story [Arrival of the Dutch]; Snake, included with Rementer, Letters on Delaware Folklore, 18 June 1991; Unami text and

trans.; W. Okla.; Bessie Snake; 350 words. When the whites came, they promised to treat the Lenape well "as long as the creek flows and our uncle the sun moves and . . . the grass grows." In exchange for a red flag the whites agreed to take a piece of land as big as a cowhide. But they cut the hide (into strips?) and thus took a large piece (cf. DIDO'S PURCHASE OF CARTHAGE). Whites then gave an ax and a hoe, which the Lenape wore as a necklace; whites showed the Lenape how to use the implements to cut trees and make houses.

216. The Story of Mahtahis [PETITIONERS SELECT MAGICAL ATTRIBUTES with motif Would-be womanizer punished]; Rementer, Letters on Delaware Folklore, 11 Feb. 1992; col. 23 Jan. 1992; W. Okla.; Esther Homovich; 580 words. Men find bones of a monster and burn the bones while each makes a wish. Among the suggested wishes: long life, good hunting, healthy children. But Mahtahis, who usually stays home with the women while the men hunt, rejects these suggestions and wishes for women "to fight over me till I die." As he wishes, so it is granted. Women literally tear him apart.

217. Why the Crane Has a Long Neck; Rementer, Letters on Delaware Folklore, 11 Feb. 1992; col. 24 Jan. 1992; W. Okla.; Marvine Parton Watkins; 230 words. Crane tells his wife he is about to die and instructs her to bury him alive. Later the deceitful Crane is found with a new woman friend. When his wife catches him, she pulls his neck. Thus the crane today has a long neck.

218. Why the Dove Builds a Nest the Way He Does; Rementer, Letters on Delaware Folklore, 11 Feb. 1992; col. 24 Jan. 1992; W. Okla.; Marvine Parton Watkins; 160 words. When the Lord was teaching the birds to build nests, the know-it-all dove flew off before the lesson was finished. Thus the dove builds a flimsy nest.

PART THREE : Stories of Uncertain Origin

Stories here regarded as doubtfully Delaware are reviewed using the same format as in Part Two.

A. [WOMAN WHO FELL FROM THE SKY]; Van der Donck, pp. 107–9; pub. 1656 per Weslager, *History;* Yonkers? (but this might have been collected at Albany and might therefore be Mahican or even Mohawk). All was water; a pregnant woman fell from heaven and settled into the water. Immediately some land appeared under her and increased; trees grew. The woman brought forth animal triplets: deer, bear, and wolf, then cohabited with them. From this, all men and animals are descended—timid like the deer, brave like the bear, or deceitful like the wolf. The woman returned to the sky, where she dwells with "God." Retold in J. A. Jones, *Traditions,* 2:93–98. *Note:* Brinton, p. 136, paraphrases this "Mohegan" myth and adds that it is "followed by a migration myth" to the effect that forefathers came out of the northwest from a tidewater area and traveled far until they reached another tidewater, the Hudson River (but Brinton must here be referring to the narrative of Hendrick Aupaumut; see ibid., p. 20).

B. Walam Olum; Rafinesque, "Walamolum," text, pictographs, and trans., redrawn and transcribed in Brinton; 1820 for the sticks, 1822 for the text per Brinton, p. 153; purportedly Indiana (but see note 32 to the Introduction, this volume). The Great Spirit was in the fog; made land and sky, sun, moon, stars; gave the first mother, gave fish, beasts, birds (recalls Genesis 1); but an evil being made monsters, noxious insects (GOOD AND EVIL CREATORS). All beings were friendly. Then an evil being, a mighty magician, brought discord (Brinton, p. 166, sees variant of Heckewelder's GOLDEN DAYS). Evil serpent caused DELUGE; survivors escaped to turtle (cf. TURTLE ISLAND), where NANABUSH banished flood and serpent (some Canadian Munsee say Nanapush instructed the earth diver, other Munsee say this is Ojibwa influence—Harrington, "Sketch," p. 232) (cf. Ojibwa serpent-and-flood myths). Myth is followed by MIGRATION ACROSS OCEAN and MIGRATION FROM THE WEST.

C. The Long Fast or The Indian Chief Turned to a Robin: A Legend of the Missouri; Adams, *Legends,* pp. 30–33; pub. 1905; story of a "Delaware" youth turned into a robin, attributed to "M. Hopewell, London, 1874," but evidently derived from Schoolcraft (see M. Williams, *Schoolcraft,* p. 106, "Iadilla or the Origin of the Robin: From the Odjibwa").

D. [Creation, DELUGE, EARTH DIVER]; Harrington, *Dickon,* p. 282–85; evidently adapted by Harrington from the Mississauga Ojibwa myth in P. Jones, *History,* pp. 33–35, and in Waubuno, pp. 8–9 (note that Waubuno reprints the myth after Jones, without attribution, merely changing the deity's name from Nanabush to Amen-a-push and calling the tale a Munsee tradition). The Creator made the earth and put creatures on it, including the toad, which regulated water (Algonquian motif: Batrachian is master of water—also Malecite, Micmac). Horned serpent gores toad, releasing water and causing world FLOOD. NANABUSH (also called Amenapush) saves animals by climbing a tree that stretches, makes a raft, sends forth the EARTH DIVER, chooses the turtle to hold the earth (TURTLE ISLAND), blows on the earth, sends a wolf to see if the expanding earth is big enough.

E. [ORIGIN OF AUTUMN HAZE]; Harrington, *Dickon,* p. 285; evidently adapted by Harrington from the Mississauga Ojibwa myth in P. Jones, *History,* p. 35. After re-creating the earth, NANABUSH retires to the far north, sleeps in winter like a bear, smokes his pipe in fall, thus causing autumn haze.

F. A Dispute Between the Spirits [North Wind and Sun]; Rementer, ed., Christmas letters, Unami text and trans.; E. Okla.; Nora Dean. Essentially the same as G, below. *Note:* Rementer says this text was put into Lenape by Nora Dean after a story in English handed to her by a student; Rementer doubts it is a traditional Delaware tale (personal communication).

G. North Wind and Sun; Hale, *Cooley's,* p. 55, Unami text and trans.; col. 1977–80; W. Okla.; Willard Thomas; 110 words. North Wind and Sun argue over which of them can make a man remove his blanket. Wind blows furiously, but the man only wraps the blanket tighter around him. Sun shines hot, and the man removes it. Sun is the winner.

H. [Crow obtains fire]; Van Laan, *Rainbow Crow,* purportedly retold after Bill "Whippoorwill" Thompson, a "Lenape elder" whom Van Laan met in Bucks County, Pa.; pub. 1989. When the animals were freezing, Crow brought fire, scorching his feathers; thus the crow is black. Perhaps derived ultimately from James Mooney, "Myths of the Cherokees" (*Nineteenth Annual Report of the Bureau of American Ethnology,* pp. 240–41).

PART FOUR : Comparative Notes

Delaware tale types and motifs recurring outside Delaware tradition—CAPITALIZED here and elsewhere in this Guide—are listed below with their non-Delaware sources. Note that particular attention is paid to Algonquian and Iroquoian materials, since these cultures are related to the Delaware either genetically or geographically. In other words, no Algonquian or Iroquoian references have been intentionally omitted (except in the case of universal motifs), whereas references from farther afield have been included selectively.

Following the definitions given by Stith Thompson in his standard work *The Folktale* (p. 414), a tale, or "type," is "made up of a number of motifs in a relatively fixed order and combination," the motif being "the smallest element in a tale having a power to persist in tradition." Seemingly clear as stated, the distinction between tale and motif is sometimes hard to keep. For this reason an intermediate category, "tales freely based on a single strong motif," has been introduced to account for the second of the three sections below.

All types and motifs treated in the present work are here regarded as Native American, uninfluenced by Old World lore, unless otherwise indicated. In a few cases the biblical Old Testament is apparently the ultimate source, as noted. Where "Aarne-Thompson" types are cited, an Old World folkloric source is at least a possibility. Items tagged "universal" (with a Thompson *Motif-Index* citation) are of worldwide distribution, not reliably traceable to either hemisphere.

Numerals in square brackets at the end of each entry refer to the abstracts in Part Two, where the type or motif in question may be found in its Delaware context.

For clarification, it should be added that this brief catalog harks back to the pre-Thompson era of American Indian folkloristics, when pioneering students such as Franz Boas and Gladys Reichard felt free to recognize types not previously described and to devise new catchwords to designate them. After Thompson's great work of classification, there came to be a tacit agreement among folklorists that types and motifs were now permanently established. Unfortunately, as more folklore collections became available, especially from the Americas, Thompson's limited (even if vast) system began falling into disuse, perhaps because it had become inadequate to describe the material. Thompson's system deserves to be revived and expanded—or, at least, used flexibly, as has been attempted here.

Tale Types

BEAR BOY. Boy adopted by bear and raised with her cubs is later restored to human society; some variants open with an episode in which the boy is abused by his father or guardian, who abandons him in the woods.

With abused-boy episode. CAYUGA: Waugh, notebook 6, p. 16. ONONDAGA: Beauchamp, p. 51. SENECA: Cornplanter, p. 167; Curtin and Hewitt, "Seneca Fiction," no. 66; A. C. Parker, no. 18; Smith, p. 44. TUSCARORA: Rudes and Crouse, p. 224. WYANDOT: Barbeau, nos. 35–38. [60, 87]

Without abused-boy episode. MALECITE: Mechling, no. 29; Speck and Hadlock, p. 364. MICMAC: Rand, p. 259. MISTASSINI CREE: A. Tanner, p. 148. MONTAGNAIS-NASKAPI: Speck, *Naskapi,* p. 108. PENOBSCOT: Leland and Prince, p. 239; Speck, "Penobscot Tales," p. 85, and *Penobscot Man,* p. 217. SENECA: Smith, p. 42. [116, 121, 122, 131, 174]

BRIDE AND THE BROTHERS. Somewhat variable type called "Mudjikiwis" in Thompson (*Tales,* p. 334), called "The Red Swan" in Bierhorst (*Mythology of North America,* p. 252), with listings for CREE, FOX, MENOMINEE, OJIBWA, ONONDAGA, OMAHA, OSAGE, etc. Regarding the Delaware variant see, especially, SENECA: Curtin and Hewitt, "Seneca Fiction," no. 111; A. C. Parker, no. 20. [71]

DRUNKENNESS OF NOAH. OLD TESTAMENT: Gen. 9:20–27. Angry that his son Ham has looked upon him in his drunkenness, Noah curses Ham's descendants, decreeing that they will be the slaves of his other two sons' descendants. Widely adapted in European and Euro-American lore to explain the origin of races (for discussion see Genovese, p. 245). Cf. ORIGIN OF THE THREE RACES. [33, 37, 213; cf. 128, 135]

EARTH DIVER. Animal dives through primal waters and brings up mud to form the earth. Widespread in North America; for extensive bibliography (including CHEROKEE, IROQUOIS, OJIBWA, OTTAWA) see Thompson, *Tales,* p. 279, and Bierhorst, *Mythology of North America,* p. 255. Also, MISSISSAUGA OJIBWA: P. Jones, p. 34. SHAWNEE: Trowbridge, in Kinietz and Voegelin, p. 60ff.; Voegelin, *Shawnee Female Deity,* p. 9. [9, 30, 65, 77, 187]

FALL OF THE ANGELS. Widespread in European and American lore, apparently derived from OLD TESTAMENT: Isaiah 14 and Luke 10:18; for discussion see Leach and Fried, p. 650, s.v. "Lucifer." [27, 35]

FORTUNATE HUNTER. Hunter repeatedly bags game without intending to do so (similar but not clearly related to Aarne-Thompson type 1640–III: Lucky Hunter). CHEROKEE: Kilpatrick, pp. 101–4. NATCHEZ: Swanton, *Myths and Tales,* pp. 262–64. SENECA: Myrtle, pp. 116–20 (with motif FORTUNATE HUNTER FLIES WITH GEESE). [51, 192]

HUNTERS AND THE WATER MONSTER. SHAWNEE: Trowbridge, in Schutz, pp. 147–49; Voegelin, in Schutz, pp. 149–54 (with FISHED-UP TURTLE); Office of Indian Affairs *Bulletin,* in Schutz, p. 162. [78, 141, 191; cf. 163]

LITERAL FOOL KILLS SLEEPING BABY. Instructed to keep flies off baby, foolish baby-sitter swats and kills baby; tries to hide from baby's mother by disguising himself as a duck or goose. WYANDOT: Barbeau, no. 69. Cf. MAN WHO MISUNDERSTANDS. [106]

MOTHER OF GHOSTS. SENECA: Curtin and Hewitt, "Seneca Fiction," no. 116. [200]

ORIGIN OF PLEIADES. People, often children, typically subjected to fasting, hunger, or food shortages, rise to become a star cluster; some variants include an intermediate or final transformation that yields one or more pines or cedar trees (TREE motif). Widespread in North America; for bibliography (including CHEROKEE, IROQUOIS, WYANDOT) see Thompson, *Tales,* p. 291. Also, NATCHEZ: Swanton, *Myths and Tales,* p. 242 (with TREE motif). [26, 120, 123, 134; with TREE motif: 80, 102, 103. Cf. 145, 157, 171, 185]

ORIGIN OF THE THREE RACES. God made the black race, but it was too dark; red race, still too dark; white, pale enough. In some Delaware versions (also Seneca) the whites are too pale, the red race just right. SENECA: Curtin and Hewitt, "Seneca Fiction," no. 30. Cf. DRUNKENNESS OF NOAH. *Note:* A somewhat different tale, not recorded for the Delaware, may be styled "Destiny of the Three Races": in an Ojibwa version given by Warren (p. 58), the Great Spirit made the three races from earth, gave a book to the whites, signifying wisdom; a hoe to the blacks, for servitude; a bow to the red race, signifying the hunter state. [33, 37, 213; cf. 128, 135]

ORPHEUS. A grieving mortal is permitted to retrieve a loved one from the dead land but again loses the beloved, this time permanently, upon breaking a certain prohibition. Widespread in North America; for bibliography (including CHEROKEE and IROQUOIS) see Thompson, *Tales,* p. 337); for extended discussion see Hultkranz. [163]

PETITIONERS SELECT MAGICAL ATTRIBUTES. A supernatural grants seekers' requests; immoderate request provokes punishment. For bibliography of ASSINIBOINE, FOX, MALECITE, MENOMINEE, MICMAC, OJIBWA, PASSAMAQUODDY, POTAWATOMI, SAUK, and other sources see Fisher, pp. 239, 253–61; and Thompson, *Tales,* p. 276: Deity grants requests to visitors. Also, SHAWNEE: Schutz, p. 162. [126, 161, 216]

RACES. See ORIGIN OF THE THREE RACES.

SERPENT'S BRIDE. Young woman marries man who turns out to be a dangerous serpent. SENECA: Curtin and Hewitt, "Seneca Fiction," no. 51; A. C. Parker, no. 26. TUNICA: Swanton, "Louisiana and Texas," p. 288. WYANDOT: Barbeau, no. 5. [86, 202; cf. 143]

THREE RACES. See ORIGIN OF THE THREE RACES.

TOWER OF BABEL. OLD TESTAMENT: Gen. 11. Thompson (*Tales,* p. 360) cites CHOCTAW and PAPAGO variants. [81, 137, 199]

WOMAN WHO FELL FROM THE SKY. HURON, IROQUOIS, SHAWNEE, and WYANDOT variants are cited in Thompson, *Tales,* p. 278; and Bierhorst, *Mythology of North America,* p. 250. [10, 11, 14, 15, 30, 44, 45, 46]

Tales Freely Based on a Single Strong Motif

ANCESTORS EMERGE FROM UNDERWORLD. Widespread in North America; for extensive bibliography (including IROQUOIS, MENOMINEE, NANTICOKE, POWHATAN, and WYANDOT) see Wheeler-Voegelin and Moore. Also, MOHAWK: Pyrlaeus, in Heckewelder, *History,* p. 251. ONONDAGA: Canassatego, in Boyd, p. 51. SENECA: Myrtle, p. 107. [18, 21]

CORN SPIRIT, OFFENDED. See OFFENDED CORN SPIRIT.

CROW BRINGS CORN. NARRAGANSETT: R. Williams, p. 85. SENECA: Converse, p. 63. [5]

GOOD AND EVIL CREATORS. Universal motif (Thompson, *Motif-Index,* A50). Familiar Iroquois theme; see, e.g, Curtin and Hewitt, "Seneca Fiction," p. 462; Hewitt, "Iroquoian Cosmology," first part, pp. 187–96, 302–26. [152; cf. 44–46]

JACK THE NUMSKULL. See MAN WHO MISUNDERSTANDS.

LOSS OF THE ANCIENTS. An ancient race is destroyed, is buried, or disappears. Widespread motif in Latin American Indian lore; see Bierhorst, *Mythology of Mexico and Central America.* Also, ARIKARA: Dorsey, *Arikara,* no. 3. PAWNEE: Dorsey, *Pawnee,* p. 134; Grinnell, *Pawnee,* pp. 355–56. [144]

MAN WHO MISUNDERSTANDS. Eccentric protagonist misapplies ambiguous instructions and bungles every time; yet, in some variants (Delaware, Wyandot), he is magically powerful. Probably related, at least in part, to Aarne-Thompson types 1692 (The Stupid Thief) and 1693 (The Literal Fool); see also Thompson, *European Tales,* pp. 416–26, "Jack the Numskull" and "Jack the Trickster." CAYUGA: Waugh, notebook 5, p. 40. MICMAC: Rand, no. 57. ONONDAGA: Waugh, notebook 14, p. 30. SENECA: A. C. Parker, no. 17; Smith, p. 50. WYANDOT: Barbeau, no. 68. Cf. CHINOOK: Boas, p. 158. TILLAMOOK: Jacobs, p. 188. See also LITERAL FOOL KILLS SLEEPING BABY, above. [23, 49, 50, 79, 97, 106, 107 127, 149, 150, 155, 156, 167, 169]

MIGRATION ACROSS OCEAN. Ancestors migrate across wide water (said to have been frozen in Delaware, Nanticoke, Shawnee, and Tuscarora traditions). ALABAMA: Schutz, p. 171; Swanton, *Myths and Tales,* p. 118. CHEYENNE: Dorsey, in Thompson, *Tales,* p. 264; Stands in Timber, pp. 13–14. HICHITI: Swanton, *Early History,* p. 173. NANTICOKE: Beatty, in Brinton, p. 139; Beatty?, in Schutz, p. 123; Loskiel, pt. 1, p. 24; Zeisberger, p. 132. OJIBWA: Mallery, p. 566, "from an island." SHAWNEE: Schutz, pp. 22, 24, 33, 34, 47, 48 (with EXPANDING BOAT motif), 55, 58, 70–71, 73, 119–32, etc. TUSCARORA (but possibly derived from an Algonquian source): Wallace and Reyburn. [81, 198]

MIGRATION FROM THE WEST. MAHICAN: Skinner, "Notes," pp. 101–2. NANTICOKE: Beatty, in Brinton, p. 138. [16]

OFFENDED CORN SPIRIT. Female corn spirit withdraws, offended by human irreverence. Widespread motif, especially in North American Southwest and Mexico. CAYUGA: Waugh, notebook 8, p. 33. SENECA: Curtin and Hewitt, "Seneca Fiction," no. 121; A. C. Parker, no. 24. SHAWNEE: Voegelin, *Shawnee Female Deity,* p. 7. [67, 117]

ORIGIN OF AUTUMN HAZE. Caused by supernatural's pipe smoke. MISSISSAUGA OJIBWA: P. Jones, p. 35. [124]

TRIBES SEPARATE OVER TRIVIAL INCIDENT. Widespread in North America; for extensive bibliography (including CROW, HIDATSA, KICKAPOO, MENOMINEE, SHAWNEE) see Hadlock; also, Witthoft, "Grasshopper," p. 301. [31]

TURTLE WHO CARRIED THE PEOPLE. Giant turtle carries people into deep water. CADDO: Dorsey, *Caddo,* no. 47. CHEYENNE: Marriott and Rachlin, p. 60. CREEK: Swanton, *Myths and Tales,* p. 36. SHAWNEE (with FISHED-UP TURTLE motif): Trowbridge, in Kinietz and Voegelin, p. 43; C. F. Voegelin, in Schutz, pp. 149, 151; Anonymous, in Schutz, p. 161. [93]

WHITE MAN CREATED FROM FOAM. ONONDAGA: Hewitt, "Iroquoian Cosmology," second part, p. 523. YUCHI: Speck, *Yuchi,* p. 150. [85, 180]

WHY DOGS SNIFF ONE ANOTHER. Cf. Aarne-Thompson types 200A (Why Dogs Look at One Another Under the Tail, Europe) and 200B (Why Dogs Sniff at One Another, eastern Europe). Also cf. CAKCHIQUEL (Guatemala): Redfield, p. 256—to safeguard the deed of title to their house while crossing a river, three dogs arrange for one of them to carry the title in his rectum; when the far shore is reached, the other two sniff the carrier to find the deed; thus dogs to this day sniff one another. [159, 168, 179]

Motifs

CANNIBAL. See STONE GIANT, STUPID GIANT, WINTER CANNIBAL.

CREATION BY THOUGHT. Deity creates by merely thinking (sporadic American Indian motif). Sporadic universal motif (Thompson, *Motif-Index,* A612). [25]

DANIEL IN THE LIONS' DEN. OLD TESTAMENT: Dan. 6. [129]

DELUGE. Universal motif (Thompson, *Motif-Index,* A1010). [9, 65; cf. 136]

DIDO'S PURCHASE OF CARTHAGE. According to a well-known anecdote, to which Vergil alludes in the Aeneid, Bk. 1, line 368, Dido negotiated the purchase of as much land as a bull's hide would cover, then cut the hide into strips to make a rope that encompassed a large district; for discussion see Rose, p. 309. WYANDOT: Barbeau, nos. 90, 91. Cf. LAND SALE WITH CHAIR DECEPTION. [17, 40, 83, 203, 215]

DOG GUARDS ROUTE TO AFTERWORLD. Widespread motif in Mexico and in Central and South America (see Benson). Similar but presumably not related to Thompson, *Motif-Index,* A673: Hound of hell. MIAMI: Trowbridge, in Kinietz, "Meearmeear," p. 52. OJIBWA: Goodsky, pp. 206–7; J. Tanner, p. 289. POTAWATOMIE: Jenness, p. 109. SHAWNEE: Howard, p. 167; Schutz, p. 97. [151, 194]

DYING BROTHER. Culture hero weeps inconsolably over the death of his brother; in some versions the brother becomes lord of the underworld. For bibliography of ASSINIBOIN, BLACKFEET, CREE, FOX, MONTAGNAIS, MENOMINEE, OJIBWA, OMAHA, POTAWATOMI, and SAUK sources see Bierhorst, *Mythology of North America,* p. 252. [46]

ETERNAL WEAVER. World will end when woman-spirit's weaving, unraveled each night, is at last complete. SENECA: Curtin and Hewitt, "Seneca Fiction," p. 625. SHAWNEE: Voegelin, *Shawnee Female Deity,* p. 21; Howard, pp. 165–66, 168; Schutz, p. 64. [201]

EXPANDING BOAT. See MIGRATION ACROSS OCEAN.

FISHED-UP TURTLE. See HUNTERS AND THE WATER MONSTER.

FORTUNATE HUNTER FLIES WITH GEESE. See FORTUNATE HUNTER.

GIANT. See STONE GIANT, STUPID GIANT.

GOLDEN AGE. Formerly there was no war, no disease, no death, etc. Universal motif (Thompson, *Motif-Index,* A1101.1). [19]

HARE AS DEMIURGE (called NANABUSH in some Algonquian traditions). For bibliography (including IOWA, MENOMINEE, OJIBWA, OMAHA, WINNEBAGO) see Bierhorst, *Mythology of North America,* pp. 213–14, 252. Also, MISSISSAUGA OJIBWA: P. Jones, p. 33. POWHATAN: Strachey, p. 102. [11, 44, 45]

HUMANS CREATED FROM TREE OR LOG. NORTHEAST: Kalm, p. 686. PASSAMAQUODDY: Leland, p. 18. [2]

INEXHAUSTIBLE FOOD SUPPLY. Universal motif (Thompson, *Motif-Index,* D1652.1). For extensive North American bibliography (including MENOMINEE, MICMAC, OJIBWA, SENECA, WYANDOT) see Thompson, *Tales,* p. 336. Also, SHAWNEE: Voegelin, *Shawnee Female Deity,* p. 5. [201]

JONAH. Human swallowed by monster. Universal motif (Thompson, *Motif-Index,* F911.4). [41]

LAND SALE WITH CHAIR DECEPTION. Europeans negotiate purchase of as much land as a chair will cover, then unwind cording from the chair seat to encompass a large district. SHAWNEE: Trowbridge, in Kinietz and Voegelin, p. 10. Cf. DIDO'S PURCHASE OF CARTHAGE. [22, 28]

LIQUOR TRIED FIRST ON THE AGED. Suspicious of Europeans' gift of alcohol, Indians allow their aged to try it first, because the aged are soon to die anyway. OJIBWA: Warren, p. 120. [28, 40]

MAGIC PARTING OF WATERS. Universal motif (Thompson, *Motif-Index,* D1551, and *Tales,* p. 276). CHEYENNE: Dorsey, in Thompson, *Tales,* p. 264. SHAWNEE: Trowbridge, in Schutz, p. 24—"water was dried up." [81]

MARRIAGE OF THE NORTH AND THE SOUTH. For bibliography of NORTHWEST COAST and CHEROKEE references see Thompson, *Tales,* p. 288. [34, 39]

MIGRATION IN EXPANDING BOAT. See MIGRATION ACROSS OCEAN.

NANABUSH. See HARE AS DEMIURGE.

RESUSCITATION BY FRIGHTENING DEAD. For bibliography of CROW, MENOMINEE, OJIBWA, PAIUTE, and SENECA sources see Thompson, *Tales,* p. 319. Also, BLACKFEET: Grinnell, *Blackfeet,* p. 141. SHAWNEE: Trowbridge, in Schorer, "Man Eater Spirit," p. 318. [71]

RISING AND FALLING SKY. For bibliography of SENECA and other sources see Thompson, *Tales,* p. 275. [13]

SPLIT BODY IN SKY WORLD. Supernatural being, half black and half red, dwells in sky. ONONDAGA: Fenton, pp. 104–5; Hewitt, "Iroquoian Cosmology," second part, p. 792. SENECA: Curtin and Hewitt, "Seneca Fiction," no. 119; A. C. Parker, no. 2. [88]

STONE GIANT. Cannibal giant has impenetrable stonelike skin. Characteristic Iroquoian motif; see, e.g., SENECA: Beauchamp, p. 146; Curtin and Hewitt, "Seneca Fiction," nos. 12, 34, 47, 48, 58, etc.; A. C. Parker, no. 55; Smith, p. 16. WYANDOT: Barbeau, no. 8. Note close relationship to WINTER CANNIBAL, q.v. [204]

STUPID GIANT. Universal motif (Thompson, *Motif-Index,* G501: Stupid ogre). CREE, MICMAC, and MONTAGNAIS-NASKAPI sources are cited by Fisher, p. 248. [144]

TOOTHED BALL STICKS TO TREE. SHAWNEE: Trowbridge, in Schorer, "Man Eater Spirit," pp. 313–14. Note similarity to the Central Algonquian motif ANIMAL-HEAD BALL; see Skinner, "Some Aspects," p. 98. Also cf. Passamaquoddy skull-ball with snapping jaws, in Prince, "Passamaquoddy Texts," p. 35. [71]

TREE. See ORIGIN OF PLEIADES.

TURTLE, FISHED-UP. See HUNTERS AND THE WATER MONSTER, PEOPLE WHO RODE THE TURTLE.

TURTLE ISLAND. Earth is formed on the back of a turtle. For bibliography of ARAPAHO, GROS VENTRE, HURON, IROQUOIS, MANDAN, OJIBWA, and SHAWNEE sources see Bierhorst, *Mythology of North America,* p. 250; and Thompson, *Tales,* p. 279. [2, 30, 44–46, 65, 77, 78]

TURTLE WINS RACE. Universal motif (cf. Thompson, *Motif-Index,* K11.3: Hare and tortoise race). [193]

TWIN SONS. Universal motif (Thompson, *Motif-Index,* T685: Twins). For bibliography of Twin adventurers motif (including CHEROKEE, FOX, MICMAC, and SENECA) see Thompson, *Tales,* p. 320. [10, 11, 14, 15, 44–46]

VOICE OF YOUNG THUNDER. Youngest of the thunder spirits has a different voice. CHEROKEE: Witthoft and Hadlock, p. 418. SENECA: Curtin and Hewitt, "Seneca Fiction," nos. 28, 43; Cf. Converse, pp. 42–45. [42, 139, 164; cf. 86]

WHITE DEER. SENECA: Curtin and Hewitt, no. 50. [43]

WINTER CANNIBAL. Cannibal associated with ice, snow, or far north. OJIBWA: Barnouw, pp. 120–31 and 155–227 passim. PASSAMAQUODDY: Leland, p. 246; Prince, "Passamaquoddy Texts," p. 33. PENOBSCOT: Speck, "Penobscot Tales," p. 14. SHAWNEE: Converse, p. 74. [126, 144; cf. 204]

TEXTS

The two principal collections of Delaware folklore that have remained in archives awaiting publication are those made by M. R. Harrington, 1907–10, and by Truman Michelson, 1912. The Harrington papers, now at the National Museum of the American Indian in New York, were not accessible until 1989; the Michelson papers, at the Smithsonian Institution in Washington, have been accessible for some years but have remained little known beyond a small group of specialists. The pages that follow include all the previously unpublished myth and folktale texts from these two collections. Text numbers assigned in the Guide, Part Two, have been retained. Thus texts 67, 70, 73–75, 78–80, 84, and 85 are from Harrington's papers;[1] *93–98, 100, and 101 are from Michelson's.*[2]

All texts in this section appear to be from Unami sources—either demonstrably or presumably from Oklahoma—except 74 and 101, which are from the Munsee. All are preserved in English only, except 95 and 101, translated from the Unami and the Munsee, respectively.[3]

In the editing of these narratives, paragraphing has been added and punctuation amended for ease of reading. Spelling has not been changed except to correct obvious and unimportant slips.

Text 101, a factual account of the Munsee westward migration, is evidently history, not legend, but is included here for comparison with other, folkloric accounts of Delaware wanderings.

67

Disappearance of Mother Corn

Corn was said to be a living Spirit. In days of old some young boys, making light of the idea of Corn being humanlike, said to one another, "Corn could not possibly leave the earth." Then the Corn disappeared and before them was the danger of great famine staring them in the face, much to their regret.

At this time some person was blessed with a token from the Great Spirit, saying, "Unless they could find someone who had the gift or power to communicate with the Spirit of Corn and coax to humor the Corn that it might return, it would cause a continual famine."

When that Corn began to disappear, the heart of Corn turned into living beings, and all began disappearing in flight with wings.

A man who had communicated with the great Spirit was told, by token, the cause of the loss of Corn and all other vegetables was because the boys or young men had made unnecessary remarks about the Corn and its Spirit, therefore the Misingw or "whole face," being the leading Spirit, was sent with the token to warn members of the tribe [of] the great wrong the young men had committed, in their estimation.

One man is quoted as saying that corn could not get away from him, and he filled a great skin bag and always placed it under his head at nighttime, when he suddenly realized that his sack had disappeared, went to flight in form of a weevil.

It was a great mystery as to who could restore Mother Corn.

They had learned that there was two boys very poor and needy who lived with scant means. They being informed of the conditions, they came to the great gathering of the people, where they offered their services to restore Corn. They possessed the mystic power and spirit.

At the gathering the Indians were sitting in a ring, when the boys departed at nighttime, not leaving any clue as to how. But when the boys reached the great region above, there they made a burnt offering out of mussel shell, sacrificing the shells for the return of Corn. Mother Corn said she would return by request of the boys who were sent. They returned and brought the glad tidings, each bringing with them a handful of Corn and the pledge that Corn would never leave again. It is supposed that these boys took flight like the Corn.

The Corn famine had been in progress one year before the people found by what means they could induce the Corn to return and did induce her by the influence of the two boys. Upon coming to the region above, the boys found the Spirit Corn was in the image of an aged woman appearing to be a scabby person, indicating that it was because the people had misused her. She said, "When Corn was being ofttimes parched, my children did me this great wrong. There are other ways to handle me. For instance, use tallow or other means to moisten me."

When they visited her, it was then they made the burnt offering of the shells. Mother Corn refusing to come back to earth at first, they went away in distress but by the sacrifice with the shells, they brought Mother Corn. She wanted to partake of the offering, but was refused unless she would promise to return in the required time to earth, to which she finally consented.

It was God's will that the Spirit Corn abide in the far heavenly region in image of an aged woman with dominion over all vegetation.

So this tradition comes from our forefathers, said to have happened before the discovery of this continent by the paleface, and centuries beyond. Thereby we know that Corn was here at the discovery of this continent.

The Corn was divided until quantities were again raised, and it is still retained. We are told that the mystic power possessed by the two boys is the means of getting Mother Corn to stay by the oath, to never leave this earth and her children again. She being in image of a woman, it was the custom of the red man to have the woman to care for and culture the Corn always, dressing neatly as visiting, when they were in the field to work and cultivate Corn, and in husking the same. Always they planted flour Corn and hominy Corn.

Charles Elkhair

70

Wēmatē´gŭnīs[4]

Some fellows were going out hunting, and one happened to kill a deer—the others were around, but he did not know how far. He skinned it and packed it on his back, then went on looking for these fellows.

After a while, he whooped to call them, and they answered him, seemed like close.

He ran all the time and got across the hollow, but saw nobody, then whoop[ed] again. And it kept on, the other fellow answering just across the hollow.

He threw the deer down and chased the fellow who was answering him.

It was a "little fellow," who carried a box with the bark on. And he knew him. "We'll have a fight right here," he said. "You were answering me while I thought it was the other fellows."

So the little one said, "All right, we'll fight. Wait while I pull off my coat."

When he pulled off his coat, the other was ready to fight. The little one said, "Wait until I pull off the other one."

He pulled off twelve coats this way, until he was right small.

Then the other did not want to fight him, he was so small. "But I will give you a name," [he] said. "[When] you get home, tell your folks somebody gave you a name: your name will be Answer-me, *näXko'mīnł*."

This little one said, "I wanted to see how strong you was. That is why I did that way to you."[5]

73

Why the Turtle Phratry Is Best

They say that the three persons or manlike animals who started the totems of the Lenape once had an argument about which was best. As they argued, they came to a big river, on the other side of which they could see food.

Now, the Turkey boasted he could get across to the food, and the Turtle said the same. But the Wolf had to give it up right there.

Then the Turkey took a running start and flew, but he gave out close to the other shore and fell into the water but finally managed to flounder ashore.

Meantime the Turtle just walked across underwater and got the food! (laughter) — but the wolf could do nothing but run up and down the bank and howl.

That is why they decided that the Turtle is the best, the Turkey next, and the Wolf last.

74
A Visit to the Land of Spirits

A few Minsi men started out from their settlement to find where the dead go. They traveled southwest, and finally after a long time they came to camps and houses in nice condition, well swept out and cared for—but nobody could be seen.

However, when night came, there were people all over the village talking and laughing, and the little drum was heard from some of the lodges. The travelers mixed with these people and enjoyed themselves, and one of them even took a fancy to a woman of the village and wanted to marry her. But the people explained to him that it could not be done, that they were all dead people, spirits, and that he, a living man, could not stay with them. And when daylight came, sure enough no one could be seen in the village—everything was empty again.

Then the travelers returned to their homes, all but the man who loved the ghost woman. He killed himself so that he could join her.

75
Cyclone

They say a man went out hunting with his half-grown boy, old enough to cook and watch horses.

They made a camp and the man left his boy there. [After a] while he saw a tornado going by, which seemed to be near his camp. Hurrying thither, he found the camp and his boy gone. He followed on the path of the cyclone and caught up with it. It was a person walking on his hands, with his feet in the air. He had long hair trailing the ground. And when this hair wrapped around a tree or anything, that tree had to go.

The man threatened to kill the cyclone person, but the latter promised to give back his boy and his camp and never trouble his people again if he would let him go unhurt. The man agreed. And when he went back with his boy, he found his camp back again in its place.

78

A Delaware Snake Legend

from *Julius Fouts*

Twelve men were out hunting in a party one time. Early one morning before sunup, one of them heard a turkey gobbling and followed the sound toward a small lake, about which some large cottonwoods were growing. By and by, the others killed a deer and waited for him, but he never came back to the camp.

Next morning they sent another man out to find him. But he heard the turkey gobbling and went that way, never to return.

Now, by this time the rest of the party felt sure that their comrades had been killed by something nearby—the Delawares had a medicine, or power, by which they could tell when their friends were dead, so these people knew that the two had perished.

Now, the brave man who was head of the party thought the turkey gobbling which they heard now and then had something to do with it. So he led the party down to the lake the next morning.

They got there just in time to hear the last gobble of the turkey, which seemed to be up in a great cottonwood. They looked up and saw the head of an enormous snake, up among the branches, the body of which hung down the lakeward side of the tree into the water.

As they watched, it slipped down the side of the tree and into the lake where it disappeared amidst a great boiling and bubbling of the water. Evidently this was the thing that had killed their friends.

That night they sang all night. And towards morning a great fish raised itself in the water and come toward them.

"No, you are not the one we want," they cried, and sent it back.

So they sang for a number of nights and raised many strange beings, one of which was a large turtle with trees growing on its back. When the trees raised above the water, they took some of the branches and told it, "Go back, you are not the one we want."

Finally they raised the great snake, and killed it. Then they burned its body and hunted among the ashes for bits of bone to use as medicine.

As each one took a piece, he made a wish as to what he was going to use it for.

79

Strong Man

[He oversleeps]

This fellow when young was known as a very worthless and good for nothing boy and he would sleep late every morning and wouldn't go anywhere but stay around the camp with the women.

And once the people said that they were going to hunt for scalps, and he wanted to go along. And most of the people laughed at him, for they knew he wasn't any good, but they let him go, and whenever they camp anyplace, they would have him there asleep and they would not let anyone wake him up.

And whenever he would wake up he would catch up with the rest and one evening the head brave said that tomorrow we will see some men to fight with, and that morning this strong man got up early and went with the men, and never sleep late anymore.

[He alerts the enemy; kills all but one]

They walked up on the prairie where the grass was tall and there they seen some other Indians to a distance and the chief said these are too many of them let's hide from them. They won't come right this way anyway, and so they hid.

And the people pass by and this strong man couldn't stand it any longer, and he got up out of the grass and said, "Here we are," and pointed to his breast. And so all of the Indians got up and they told him now you better throw all of them down because you hallooed at them. So he run after them and threw them down on the ground, and his people ask him why he did that. He said, "You ask me to throw them down."

Well, they told him, "We mean kill them."

Well, he took his hatchet out of his belt and said, "Why didn't you tell me that before?" and started to kill them. And this strong man killed all of the men but one. And he cut off the ears and the nose and split his hands in between his fingers and sent him home and told him to bring some more people, for he would be there when they come.

[He finds a hole]

And they went on that evening and camp, and the head brave said, "We will stay here all day tomorrow and try to kill a bear to eat, for we are getting hungry."

And next morning the brave said, "Now we will go out and try to kill a bear"—and if anybody finds a hollow tree, to halloo, or whoop, and we can get together and sure there will be a bear in it.

And they started out next morning and when they got a little ways somebody whooped and they went over and seen this strong man standing beside a big stem of grass and was looking at a hole in the grass, and they told him that was not what they mean.

"We mean a big tree."

The strong man said, "Why didn't you tell me before?"

[He drives out the bear]

And they started on a little farther and they heard someone whoop again. And when they got there [they] found a big tree, and the head brave said, "Now, who can climb up there and drive the bear out?"

The strong man said, "I can." And he climb into the hole and drove the bear out. And Bear was killed.

[He dips the turkey in the grease]

And [they] went back to camp. And that day there was one man that had a bucket, and he fried some grease and took a bark of elm tree and made a bucket. And whenever he would get lots of grease in the bucket, he would pour it into the bark bucket.

And that evening the head brave said, "Tomorrow we will hunt for turkey, for it would be good to duck it in the grease."

And [the] strong man said, "All right," and next morning they started out to hunt for turkey, and he had not been gone very far until he caught a turkey alive and took it to camp.

And the strong man was there alone, and he went to ducking the turkey into the grease until the turkey was nearly dead. And when one of the hunters came back, he saw [the] strong man running around one side of the bucket and [the] other, catching the turkey and ducking it in the grease.

And when the hunter came close the strong man said, "Will you duck this turkey awhile in the grease? I am getting tired."

And the hunter said, "That is not what they mean. They mean to kill the turkey and cook it and when done eat it and dip the cooked pieces in the grease and eat it."

And the strong man said, "Why didn't you all tell me before? I would have had that turkey cooked."

[He kills the first thing he sees]
They went home from there, and when they got home the head brave said, "Always say what you mean to this strong man. He must be a great man."

And on their way home the head brave said, "We are close to home, and now we will hunt and kill the first thing that you see"—and they all answered—"and next everbody can go home."

So [the] strong man went on and sees one of his men and run after him and killed him and went on further and seen another one of his men and he killed him. When he got home he said, "I got two men."

And afterwards he always went by himself anyplace. They wouldn't say anything to him.

80

Seven Stars

There once were eight boys. Seven could go above in the air and down in the ground, while the other could not do anything—and the old man did not know what to do with him, so he took him to an island and left him there, and the boy hallooed for his grandfather but received no reply.

He staid there three days. And finally the animals of the water felt sorry for him, and they began to ask each other who [there was] to take him back to his grandfather. So finally the big horned snake said he would.

So the snake told the boy he would take him across if he would tell him where he seen a cloud come up anywhere. So they started across, and the boy got pretty near crossing and he seen a cloud. And he told the snake, and they hurried back and the snake got out of sight.

And next day the snake came back, and the boy thought that he would not tell the snake this time. So they started, and he seen a cloud but never said anything to the snake, and he reached the bank safe and the snake was struck by lightnin'.

So the boy made friends with the lightnin' [people], and they told him he would be a ruler someday and be a great man.

Those other seven boys got so they couldn't stay with their parents. There was a hill just a little way from the house, and those boys went to the hill and turn to stone all red. And they said, "If you want to see us, you can come here. Only clean people can come and see us."

And people went to see them often, and there was one fellow that didn't believe, and he dirty the rocks. When this was done, they left from there and went to a better place and turn into pine—nice seven pine trees—and said, "This is the place you want to come and see us."

There were lots of people that come and see them and lay under the shade trees, and [so] the seven found that they couldn't be trees and went up above and turn to be stars, and they said, "You people can always see us up above. We will watch the frosts. In the spring when you cannot see us in the west, there won't be any more frosts. And in the fall you can see us in the east. So you know that it is getting cold and frosts appear. We will always be in the skies and never change to another."

84

The Big Fish

There was one time an old lady who had a little granddaughter about ten years of age. They lived right at the edge of the camps next to the creek.

The little girl played on the creek very much. And finally the old lady noticed the girl was getting big, and she was surprised and did not know what was the matter with her.

In a certain length of time the girl got sick, and the old lady watched over her every day. And so the girl had this little fish. The old lady picked up the little fish and wondered if this was her great-grandchild and took it to the swamp and put it in a horse track[6] which was full of water, and the little fish made lots of flops around there.

And that evening she went back to see about the little fish, and she saw the little fish was getting big—the horse track was large and it was still playing in it.

Next morning she went back and saw nothing but a great lake. And when the lake got big, the little girl would play around its edge and wouldn't be bothered. But when any other person would go near this lake, it would be the last they were ever heard of.

And the people decided that it was the fish that was killing all of the people, so the chief called a council and try to find someone to kill the fish.

There were lots of people there who said that they couldn't[7] kill the fish. The council lasted for two or three days. Nobody would say that he could kill the fish.

There lived on the edge of the camps an old Indian woman with her two grandchildren, who were boys. For that is the way the Indians camp—the poor class of people camped at the edge of the camps. The old lady attended the councils every day and finally the largest boy ask his grandmother why she was gone every day.

This made her angry, and she picked up a stick used for the poker and hit the boy on the head and said, "What is the use of you boys to know where I go every day. You couldn't do anything. There is a big fish in the lake which is killing everybody who goes near the lake, and you boys couldn't kill him."

And the boy spoke up, "We can kill that fish. We know who he is."

And next morning the old lady went back to the council and told the chief that her grandchildren could kill the fish. And the chief told the servant to go and get the boys, and he brought them to the chief, who told them, "You boys said that you can kill the fish."

The boys said, "Yes, we can." And everybody gave wampum [8] for a purse to kill the fish.

The chief said, "If you boys kill that fish, I will give you all this wampum." And the boys went with their grandmother back home.

That night the boys went to bed early, and the old lady thought she would watch the boys and see them go to sleep. She thought they were in fun about killing the fish.

The boys were just waiting for the old lady to go to sleep, so she wouldn't see them go away.

As soon as the old lady went to sleep, they started—and went as fast as thought and got to the edge of the lake, and they turned to two birds that fly fast and went to the Sun. When they reached there, the Sun asked them, "What did you come for?"

They said, "We came after your fire."

The Sun said, "You can't take my fire, you would burn the earth up, but you can take my ashes and use them for anything."

And they took a small quantity and went back in a short time. And when they come to the lake to kill the fish, they found that the fish was very powerful and could go up in the air and under the ground.

So they had to get one under the ground and the other in the air above the lake. One turned to a butterfly and the other to a sun. The butterfly got under the ground and put ashes in the pond, while the other poured ashes from the top. And the lake got to boiling and finally all went dry. Before next morning, the boys went home and to bed.

The next morning the old lady woke up and saw the boys still asleep, and she threw the cover off of the boys and said, "You boys told a story about killing that fish. Here you are asleep!"

And they told her to look over and see if she could see any lake, and she looked and could see nothing but ashes and the big fish laying in the middle. And everyone went over and saw the fish and the chief gave the boys the wampum.

The boys had [had] to parch corn and eat it by the fire, but now they live good and have plenty.

85

Creation of the White Man

They say that the origin of the white man came in the early life of the Delaware Indians. When the white man was first created, there was no other natives then on earth except the Indians.

At this time they were visited by a man of an unknown nation, who began to teach the Indians a religion, telling them how they should live, et cetera. And this stranger resembled the Indians themselves in color and disposition.

Then the stranger departed from the Indians, going towards a nearby stream. When he reached the stream, it was flowing nicely, and in it he saw great heaps of foam accumulated on the water—and took particular notice of this, giving the situation much study.

Now this man had been sent by God to the Indians to teach them the way to live. After meditating for a time, he decided he could create man himself out of the heaps of foam.

He then gathered some of the foam and made a man, making him like the Indians. But at the finish of his creation, this being looked fairer in color, and from that time there were men of this kind. They were strong in body and increased rapidly in population.

When they become many, he had no further influence over them. They would not heed the teachings of their creator. He could find no way to induce them to observe his commands. They became boisterous and mean, very unruly, and he could not control them. So he decided to go back to God.

And when he had journeyed until near to his destination, he met his brother near a great gorge or canyon. He told his brother that his nation of people had become unruly and disobedient to him. "I taught the way to live, but they would not heed my commands, they killed me."

His brother asked him then, "Will you give our people over to me? If you give them to me I shall teach them the way of living, and every mechanical trade and benefit to mankind, and shall make them a wise nation and provide all things for their future use."

The man then consented to give these people over to his brother, for him to teach and command to the best of his ability and power. The brother then took charge of these people and taught them all mechanical trades and industries, and then the paleface people began to learn by practice the better means of progress.

Success followed, and social life and happiness was soon established among them. But this man also taught them to scheme and how to mislead their brethren to their own satisfaction.

The creator of these people soon discovered that his brother was very much wiser than himself, and that his brother had been condemned by God because he was selfish, headstrong, and disobedient, and false to Him. It was for this reason he had offered his services to his brother to take command of the people he had created on earth, and to this day we find more evil than goodness throughout the entire world and that evil is the stronger in every respect.

This condemned man must have been Satan, who was so false to God that he could no longer arrange to stay with Him, so he was sent away to earth where he met his brother at the great gorge.

This tradition come down from our forefathers from ancient times, being handed from generation to generation until it is now with us at the present day, the teachings of which enable me to relate this story.

Julius Fouts

93

[Twelve Men on a Turtle's Back]

There was once a gang of twelve who didn't care to be sociable with any tribe of Indians. So they always wanted to go way off. Kill people. And rob them.

So these twelve one day started out to hunt some people and kill and scalp them. So they got a good ways off. They had to camp several times. They could find no trace of any human beings.

They were going along and struck a trail and wondered what in the world [it] could be. It must be a turtle.

But what a big one. It was marked flat in the ground. It was big as [a] house. They followed him up. Finally they caught up with it. They found a very large turtle.

They got on top [of] his back and examined it. All twelve were on it at once. They decided they could ride him when they went anywhere and save walking.

The turtle started when all were on his back. They kept on going several days on the turtle's back. When they got to the big water—they could see nothing but water—the turtle kept on going.

So he went straight for this big water. So when the turtle was about ready to hit the water, these men tried to jump off. But they were stuck fast. They couldn't get off.

One managed to get off before the turtle entered the water. He went back and told the people what happened. So he told them that they had found a big turtle—meanwhile they rode this turtle, this turtle went right to the big water with them—[and] he said he managed to jump off, but the others went right along with the turtle, on his back. He said, "The last I saw of them was when their heads went under the water."

So they got together and counseled over it, wondering how they could get the men back, not believing they were dead, being carried away by the turtle in the manner they were.

So. The Shawnee have always been right next to the Delawares for a long time. The Shawnee [had a man who] told the Delaware he knew of a medicine and a song with this medicine that they could use, which he thought would make the turtle come back with these men. This medicine is used principally for that purpose. It never failed.

It worked all right. All the older people and the Shawnees went with the man who showed where he had last seen the turtle with the men. So then these Shawnees and Delawares, mainly old men, camped near the water where the turtle entered the water with the eleven men.

So these Shawnees proceeded to make this medicine. They made bowls of bark. So they set this bark bowl with the medicine in it. The men sat in a half circle about, facing the water. They were on the north side. They began all to sing a song, calling this turtle to return.

During the time they were singing they heard a big roar as if some large water animal were coming. They thought it was the turtle. First, one kind of water animal appeared, and then another, [a] crayfish.

When the animal came, it would make right for that medicine and stop right where the medicine was. Then one man pushed the one [animal] back, saying, "We don't want you." Or another would appear, [and] they told him the same, as they wanted the turtle to come.

Towards the last of the other animals besides the turtle, a big snake—the largest in [the] world with long horns on his head—appeared. All kinds of lightning, all colors, was everywhere. They all said, "We've got some[thing] great this time."

"Maybe it is the turtle with the men," they said as they saw him approaching. When he came to where the medicine was and stopped and laid still, the men went up, examined him, and said he was the prettiest animal they ever saw. He was all decorated with different colors about the head.

They decided to take off some of the scales off his neck or body someplace. So when they were taking them off, [they said,] "Now we are going to take these scales off you." Some would wish one way; another, another.

Some would take a scale and put [it] in [a] split of wood. They could put that in a branch, and when the water hit it, it could be taken up, then [there] would be rain enough.[9]

Those scales are with the Delawares yet. Elkhair has one, sold one. Some would use [them] to have plenty, luck in killing deer, getting fur, et cetera.

When they got those scales off, they spoke to the snake and told him they didn't want him and pushed him back into the water.

After the snake went back, they again heard a roaring in the water. So the people knew very [well] it must be that turtle. "We have had everything else in the water come to this medicine except that turtle."

This water made all sorts [of] movements as the turtle approached. So directly they saw the turtle. Then they saw those men on his back, still living.

The turtle came right up to where this medicine was. The great chiefs then told our old man, "How shall we proceed to let him know what we want?" The old man said, "We will use tobacco. God put tobacco here on this earth to be used for this purpose, namely, whenever you want anything from animals."

So this particular old man that was selected to do this told the turtle that they didn't want him but wanted those men.

When the old man got through talking to this turtle, [he said,] "Here's tobacco that I will give you, you can take it along with you." So he tied the tobacco around the turtle's neck.

After the old man did that, these men on the turtle's back began to look around, as if they had come back to their senses the way they were before they were taken away. They saw the sun shining, and they saw the daylight.

About that time they started to get off that turtle. They walked right away from him. They saw the men sitting around. At first they hadn't, until the tobacco had been tied to the turtle's neck, for [the turtle] had taken their power away. But after he was given tobacco everything began to look natural. So the old man told the turtle that was all they wanted, so now he could go back.

Then those men who got off the turtle said that where they came from in the water everything appeared to be the same in the water—the same as it did here on the earth, except that they saw no sun. So they said they saw lots of people there, the same as here. There was some animals under the water and some people.

It was six months the men were on the turtle's back before they were brought back. This turtle took the men because he wanted the other animals to look up to him because he had other people with him.

Then all went home after the men were brought back. The Delawares still have that medicine today and use it.

94

Doll Dance

Long time ago the children were playing making dolls out of rags. Those were principally little girls that were making those dolls.

One of the little girls went out playing one day and saw a little stick and recognized that stick resembled a human being. So the little girl thought, "I'd better take this; it will make a better doll than these others."

And she got the stick, fixed it up and dressed it up like some person. It showed the very appearance of a person. So the old folks told the little girl, "Why is that you want to do this?"

"Because that wood looks more like a human being than anything else."

"The reason why we give you rags is so that you can make dolls from them." So they told the child that thing was liable to harm her sometime. So they told her to throw it away, and she did.

After she threw it away, one night this same doll appeared while she was asleep. It appeared as if it were a living person.

So this doll kept appearing to this [girl] every night when she slept. It seemed as if this doll would molest this girl in various ways, such as clutching at her throat as if to kill her. Finally the girl took sick on that account.

So they had the Indian doctors to doctor her. Through their power they discovered that that doll was the cause of that girl being sick. So these old men doctors told the parents that they would have to make a doll that resembled a human being, a live person. So they said that doll would have to be kept by the parents.

Then this old man who found out they had to make a doll and what they had to do with the doll told them that there had to be a dance to go with this doll, a stomp dance, which they would have to have take place every year.

[Text continues with ceremonial details.]

95

[Beaver, Skunk, and Owl Court a Woman]

There was a good-looking woman. Men liked her looks. But she would not have anyone.

The animals counseled about her: "I sure would like to have this woman!" Three animals—beaver, skunk, and owl—said, "Now, we'll try to get this woman."

Then they told the owl, "You go first and see her. See whether you can get this woman."

When the owl had gone to see the woman, she told him, "I wouldn't have you, you're so ugly. You've got big eyes. I wouldn't have you."

Then the owl went away. When he got back, he said, "I couldn't get that woman."

Then the skunk went next to see this woman, and she said to him, "I wouldn't have you, you're too ugly. And you stink."

Then he came back. He said, "Yes, I too could not get this woman."

Then it was the beaver's turn. He said, "Now it's my turn to get this woman." When he got there, he started to talk to the woman. But he, too, could not get the woman.

She told him, "I won't have you, you're an ugly thing. Your teeth are broad and your tail is big and broad. This tail of yours, it looks like a stirring paddle."

Then the beaver left and went back. When he got back, he said, "Well, I too could do nothing with this woman."

"Then how could we do this woman so we could get her?" They talked over how they ought to do, how they might get that woman.

Then the beaver said, "Way over here in the creek, where she gets water, there's a log that runs out into the stream. I'll go and gnaw it nearly in two. Then when she goes to fetch water, she'll break the log with her weight. She'll fall in the water, then she'll send for us to help her so she can get out."

Then, when the woman fell in, she said, "I wish Owl were here. Maybe he could help me get out of the water." Then she began to sing:

pepe kwansa
pepe kwansa
I like the beaver

But the beaver said, "No one likes my looks, because I'm ugly. My teeth are too wide and my tail too broad. My tail looks like a stirring paddle."

Then the woman kept on singing:

pepe kwansa
I like the skunk

The skunk said, "Nobody would like my looks because I'm so ugly. And because I stink."

Then again she started to sing:

pepe kwansa
I like Owl

Then the owl said, "No one likes my looks, because I'm ugly, because I've got big eyes."

Then she went down the creek, that woman. No one would help her. She finally drowned, this woman.

96

Delaware Meetinghouse

The Delaware church was given the tribe when all nations were given churches in case they wanted to live a good life and be with God. This Delaware meeting is in the beginning of spring. Then the people plant the crops. Everybody is glad because the crops are good, so in the fall they give thanks to God at this meetinghouse. For what good they have seen they attend the meetinghouse to extend it for another year. The back generation always said it has been known that this meeting [is] to be held twelve nights. They have the twelve days because the sky is divided into twelve tiers, and the Supreme Being is in the twelfth tier. So they have twelve wooden faces, [one] half black, the other [half] red. Made of sugar maple. White marks represents the eyebrows. Each represent a being not seen on earth except at certain intervals. Each can take our service[10] to the next tier till it reaches the Supreme Being. The suit is made of bearskin.

There was one time during a war, they had a war so long that the Delawares could not hold their meeting on that account. Then there was no meetinghouse. So in the meantime, the earth shook for one year. So the Delaware, not having a meetinghouse, knew of no way to check this.

So the chief has two bark houses combined. So they held their meeting there.

After they started this meeting up, all day long they shook hands with each other. The earth continually shook. Trees sank down. Directly big pools of water could be seen.

After they held the meeting for six months, the earth began to stop shaking a bit. After that in the meanwhile they built a meetinghouse like the one across the river. They held meetings in the bark house until they completed this meetinghouse. During the time they held this meeting, about March or April, at this time they held the meeting in the new meetinghouse. So one night they heard those deities represented by the wooden faces coming for several nights. Every night they come close. They could hear them hollering. So in the meetinghouse one night the older people got up and said if there's anyone here in the meetinghouse that knows those parties.[11]

So one fellow said, "Yes. I can go and talk with them. I've been gifted by them."

So two other old men went along with this fellow, and when they got over there where the wooden faces were, this fellow who said he had a gift from them asked them what they came for.[12]

So they said that God sent them down to tell the people to stop the meeting at this time, it is time to plant your corn, your garden, anything to live on—the earth had stopped shaking—and not to hold another meeting till this coming fall.

Then those false faces told those three men that hereafter they must never quit this Delaware meeting we have.

They came to assist the tribe in carrying on the meeting. Also they had control of all the deer, and these deers are to be used in carrying on the meeting. And at the time of the meeting in the fall they would drive the deer close to the meetinghouse so they could be easily found by the hunters; and for the Delawares to also make faces out of wood representing the authorities' looks identically in the faces. "So when you get the faces down representing our looks, we will put the power in them same as the power in us."

[Extensive ceremonial details are appended.]

97

Wehīx̄amōkäs[13]

[While on the warpath, he sleeps in camp]

Wehīx̄amōkäs when he was grown was very o[r]nery. He was dirty, lay down anywhere, and had no get up to him.

A bunch of Delawares went out looking for enemies. So he wanted to go along. They hardly liked to take [him] as they didn't think he amounted to anything, didn't care to be bothered with him.

They took him along.

And where they camped, he slept so long, the next morning they just left him there. So when he woke up, his men had all left him.

So he caught up with the gang of men where they were camped. When he got there he just laid down by the fire and went to sleep.

Next morning they woke up, ate their breakfast and they left him. Then again, just let him sleep. They said, "Just let him stay there."

He knew all about it beforehand and was well satisfied.

So then he caught up with them again—he got up early.

[He alerts the enemy]

Then they went on and they struck a big prairie country.

While going along they run onto a big body of men who it was impossible for them to whip. So the headman said, "We'll now have to hide in the high grass so they'll pass us and we can go on." So *Wehīx̄amōkäs,* just as he acted, squatted down as much as he could.

Every now and then he would stick his head out. "Look out, the people will see you," he was told.

So he couldn't stand it when they passed him a bit. He jumped up and beat his breast, crying out, "Here we are, we're a big body of men." There [were] only thirty [or] forty in [the] bunch, and four [or] five thousand enemies.

[He defeats the enemy single-handedly, mutilates sole survivor]

So after he did that, the others with him jumped up and told him he'd have to whip all the enemy, as he had got them started.

So then he said, "All right," and threw his blanket away.

He understood them to say, "Grab them and throw them down but don't kill them."

So he grabbed one and then another and laid them down.

So the chief told him, "That isn't what I told you to do. I told you to kill all [of] them because they're going to kill all [of] us."

And *Wehīx̄amōkäs* said, "Why in the world didn't you say so in the first place?"

And he grabbed his little ax and went right after them, till he killed every one of them with his ax but one. So the one he left was told by him, "Come here. Well, I'm going [to] cut your ears off."

He took his knife and cut his ears off, just left little pieces hanging there, cut his nose off and told him, "The rules are among men, you don't want to look good, you want to look mean. That's why I cut your ears and nose off."

So he said, "Stick out your hands." He did so. *Wehīx̄amōkäs* split his fingers far up. "Look here, did you ever notice men have long fingers? You don't look [like] a man. Your fingers are too short. That's why I split them. So he told him to go back to his people and he[14] would wait for them to come too.

[He finds a "bear" hole]

After he had done this, he and the others went on. They struck a timbered country.

They were hungry and were without anything to eat. So the chief made remarks to the crowd that they all ought to hunt bear so they would have something to eat. "Now we'll scatter out and look for a nice hole"—that's liable to be a bearhole. "If any of you find [any]thing, you must whoop, and we'll all go [to] it."

So they all started out.

Directly they heard *Wehīx̄amōkäs* hollering far off somewheres.

So he discovered a hole on a cane,[15] and [a] bird had cut that hole and lived there.

So when they got there, he said, "Here's a hole. It looks as if someone were living in there."

"My goodness, no bear can go in there!"

He told them, "Why, you ought to have told me so in the first place."

[They find a bear, and he pushes it out of its hole]

They went on from there in the usual way. Somebody whooped again. So they went over there. (It wasn't *Wehīx̄amōkäs.*) The chief said, "It's a great big tree; there's sure a bear in there. Well, is there anyone who can go up and make the bear come out of the tree?"

At that time there was always somebody who could [go] over and knock on a tree and say, "Come out," and the bear will always come. The chief thought someone would do it in the usual way.

But *Wehīx̄amōkäs* said, "Why, I can do that." So he was told, "All right."

He climbed the tree, crawled into the big hole. He went down after the bear and told the bear, "Get out of here." So directly they saw the bear come out. *Wehīx̄amōkäs* was pushing him to make him go.

[He dips a live turkey in the bear grease]

So they killed the bear. They went to a place where there was plenty of wood and camped. They skinned the bear there and barbecued it by getting a sharp stick and putting [it] pretty close to the fire.

One of the fellows made a pan of bark, and he had a bucket. He ran the bear grease into the bark pan—or the bucket. It was poured in the bark pan to cool. They camped there se[ve]ral days.

So then one of the old men said, "Tomorrow we'll hunt a turkey and dip him in this grease." So the next morning they all started to hunt those turkeys.

So *Wehīx̄amōkäs* started out with them. He struck up with a bunch of turkeys. So he did as he understood: that he would have to catch the turkey alive.

So he got after one of those turkeys and caught one alive. He took it back home to the camp. When he got there, there wasn't a soul there. He was just by himself.

The way the men spoke was to dip the turkey in grease, so he thought he would proceed with the work. So then after he got through dipping the turkey in the grease, he let him go, and after a bit would catch him again and dip him again. So he kept it up a long time as the hunters didn't return for a long time. So the turkey was grease[d] all over.

So directly he saw one of his partners coming. He was just through ducking the turkey in the grease, and this turkey was pretty nearly drowned. So he told him, "Well, I've got a turkey. I've done what you said. I'm pretty tired as I've been ducking this turkey a long time. I expect you'd better help me."

So that man said, "My goodness, you've wasted that grease, and it was sure a good grease." The turkey, by kicking, had scattered grease everyplace. "That ain't what we mean by dipping turkeys in grease. You always clean this turkey up good and cook it. Then after it's cooked you dip the meat into the grease and eat it." So *Wehīx̄amōkäs* [said,] "Why didn't you say so in the first place? I'd have had it cooked long ago."

So when the others came back, the turkey was cooked and the man told what this *Wehīx̄amōkäs* had done. The old man said, "I am going to tell you—hereafter you mustn't joke, you must talk plainly or he might play some trick on you."

[He kills a deer and heads for home alone]

So then, after that, they left that camp and went to another place to camp.

The leader said, "We ought to hunt some deer and take some deer home."

So this *Wehīx̄amōkäs* hunted for several days and killed nothing. Finally he killed a big deer.

So he had heard them say they would take the deer home. But they didn't mean that when each man killed a deer he was to go home; it was intended that when many were killed they'd all go home in a bunch.

So when he killed his deer, he skinned the deer-legs up halfway so he could tie the legs together with deer skin; he crawled under, and the deer was fastened on him.

[He throws enemies over a cliff; mutilates the sole survivor]

He went on and on. Somebody whooped. He looked around and said, "Goodness! There's a big bunch of Indians." He never stopped. Kept on going.

Those Indians surrounded him, and they said, "Well, we've got you now."

And he said, "Yes, you've got me now, I guess."

So he saw in front of him a steep cliff of rocks, probably a thousand feet to the bottom. So he commenced to go where the cliffs were.

They began to crowd about him, about to push him off. So he said, "You people must be very anxious to go down there. So I'll put you there."

He took the deer off his back and laid it down. Right then they discovered he was a man with power. They tried to get away, but they couldn't. They got plumb weak and they'd run and he'd whoop and they'd fall down. They tried to crawl on their hands and knees but couldn't.

So then he began to grab them and throw them down that steep hill. These men would stick on the limbs of trees below.

So finally he got every one, save one whom he left to tell the tale. He called him and cut [off] his ears, split his fingers. "I'm trying to make you look like a man, something mean."

[Told to hunt "everything alive," he kills two men]

In the meantime afterwards, he was going towards the camp. He threw the deer down and told his friend to skin him. They cut the deer up and camped there a few days longer. They camped three different times going back home.

So the old chief told them all the time, "You want to be careful. This man can't take a joke. The very thing you tell him, he'll go do. He may hurt us someday."

Some said, "We'll go on a hunt and kill everything alive that we see and take it home with us." So *Wehīx̄amōkäs* said, "All right."

While he was hunting, he saw one of his companions ahead. He thought, "Well, he's alive, I believe I'll get him."

So he killed him. He cut holes in his legs so he could carry him on his back.

When he went on further he saw another one of his companions. So he did the same to him, strung him up, went on home looking for anything that was alive.

When he got home, he threw the two men down in front of the people. "Well, this is all I could find alive."

The instructions were to kill anything alive.

So the old man said, "Now the thing's happened just as I told you he'd do. So now he's played this trick on us, he's killed two men. I always told you that you should explain everything fully to him so he would understand it right."

[He lives alone, kills intruders, mutilating the sole survivor]

So the chiefs notified their bands that they had discovered that he had such power he could do anything.

The chiefs told the bands hereafter to be very particular in talking to him, that when they tell him anything, they must explain it fully and kindly so he would understand it right.

At that time *Wehīx̄amōkäs* became a very powerful man. So he kind of left the tribe, and went [a] ways off, built him a bark house for himself.

One day a bunch of men came and surrounded him. They told him, "We've got you, we've got you now."

So he said, "Yes, you've got me. Come in."

He rolled the flap. They all came in. Pallets were spread down around the fire at the center of the house. "Well, sit down, men. I'll cook dinner before we go."

So he went to work and started dinner, puts some big kettles on the fire, puts lots of venison in them and water so as to make plenty of soup.

So when he got the cooking done, there was lots of boiling soup. So he asked the men, "Where's your *īla* (brave)?" They thought he was going to feed him first. So they pointed him out to him.

So he grabbed one kettle full of soup and threw the boiling soup right square on the *īla*'s face. So he had a big wooden spoon in his hand. So he dipped it in the kettles and commenced to hurl the hot soup on the others.

So they all started to run out of the house when he did that. So he kept on throwing hot soup on them and they ran out of the house as fast as they could.

After they were all out, he grabbed his little ax and he whooped at them and they all could run no further. They fell on the ground.

So he killed them all with his ax, excepting one. He cut his ears off, split his fingers—split his hands—and cut off his nose and told him to go back and tell the people, and to come back again with some people with him. "I'm going to live here all the time."

[Boy with thunderbird power becomes his partner]

So one time he went back to hunt [up] the tribe and kind of visit them.

So he came to a bark house and saw no one. So he went right in. He thought somebody might be inside.

So when he went, he saw a little boy sitting at the fireplace. He was about five [or] six years old.

So when *Wehīx̄amōkäs* stepped in, he saw the boy parching corn and eating it. So he just looked at the boy and said, "By crabs![16] You live a hard life. I'll just kill you and get you out of misery."

So he pulled out his ax, and just as he struck at him—as he got half to the boy's head—the boy disappeared, and there was a big flint rock there. *Wehīx̄amōkäs* stopped his ax. "By crabs! I came near spoiling my ax hitting that rock."

When *Wehīx̄amōkäs* got out of the notion and drew back his ax, that boy sat there again. So he said, "*Wu^e*,[17] you must be kind of powerful yourself."

So *Wehīx̄amōkäs* asked the boy who his friends were that made him so great. The thunderbirds were his friends.

So *Wehīx̄amōkäs* told him, "If the Thunderbirds are your friends, tell him to shoot that tree out there all to pieces."

So the little boy ran out, whooped, and told the Thunderbirds to strike the tree with the lightning.

So in a very short time it commenced thundering and lightening, and the lightning struck that tree and tore it all to pieces.

So the splinters scattered around and pretty nearly hit *Wehīx̄amōkäs* and scared him badly. So he told him, "You must be kind of a bully fellow yourself. So you'll be my friend hereafter," he said to the little boy.

So he picked him up and walked off with him. Finally he raised him to be a man.

[He and his young friend meet giants]

So then they would go still further by themselves. They were not afraid, as *Wehīx̄amōkäs* had a partner.

So one day *Wehīx̄amōkäs* said, "Let's go clean around this earth." So they started and went east, then north, then west; they got northwest in the cold country. They ran onto some big giants.

So those giants would follow them. A giant would whoop at them. *Wehīx̄amōkäs* then was kind of hoodooed. These people had more power than he. Every time they would holler, *Wehīx̄amōkäs* then got weaker, even his bones ached.

So this friend of his, this boy, had more power than *Wehīx̄amōkäs* had. So he helped *Wehīx̄amōkäs.* He horsewhipped *Wehīx̄amōkäs* because he was scared and was getting overpowered. So by his assistance, *Wehīx̄amōkäs* and he managed to escape from those giants.

So this friend boy told *Wehīx̄amōkäs,* "Let's go back from here. We can't go around the earth. I see those giants will kill you."

Wehīx̄amōkäs then had a grudge against his friend the boy, because the latter had more power than he had.

[Envious of boy's power, *Wehīx̄amōkäs* tries to kill him]

So then *Wehīx̄amōkäs* decided he would kill his young friend.

So then one day *Wehīx̄amōkäs* cooked a dinner, and this young man lay down beside the fire and went to sleep. *Wehīx̄amōkäs* got dinner ready. He looked at his friend. "By golly, he's asleep."

He took out his ax. "I believe I'll kill him right now."

So he struck at his head with his ax. The boy jumped away and whooped. The ax stuck in the ground. *Wehīx̄amōkäs* told him, "I just wanted to wake you. Dinner's ready."

[Boy takes revenge by chopping off *Wehīx̄amōkäs*'s headdress]

This young fellow's turn came to cook dinner one day.

So when the young man cooked dinner, *Wehīx̄amōkäs* was asleep. So this young fellow thought of what *Wehīx̄amōkäs* did to him one time when he was asleep. So he looked at *Wehīx̄amōkäs. Wehīx̄amōkäs* was sound asleep. "I could do this same to him, but he couldn't escape."

So he picked up his ax. He decided he'd do him the same way, but not kill him.

So *Wehīx̄amōkäs* was lying there with his long hair spread out. He had a headgear of deer hair and turkey's beard. This boy thought he would chop that off, and not his head. He chopped that right off.

Wehīx̄amōkäs whooped quite a piece off yonder. The young man said, "I only wanted to wake you, my friend. Dinner's ready."

So *Wehīx̄amōkäs* had kind of a grudge against this boy, because the latter had more power than he had. *Wehīx̄amōkäs* was always planning to kill him. He was in earnest when he struck at him, but the boy was only playing.

[He decapitates the boy; the boy, restored, leaves him]

So finally *Wehīx̄amōkäs* and the boy thought they'd go off to find people to kill, kind of on the warpath.

In the meanwhile, during the battles with other Indians, *Wehīx̄amōkäs* wouldn't fight in earnest with the other people. He was looking for a chance to kill his friend.

So one day while they were fighting with other Indians, *Wehīx̄amōkäs* then got a chance to hit him from behind with his ax and split his head wide open. That boy grabbed his head and put it back together the way it was before it was hit.

This boy told *Wehīx̄amōkäs,* "Well, I guess you've got me. You slipped up on me. And I didn't think you'd do me this way." So the boy told him, "I can kill you right now if I want to, but I'm not going to kill you. I'm going to let you live by yourself."

So this young man quit *Wehīx̄amōkäs* then and went home. So *Wehīx̄amōkäs* went back to where the Delawares were. So they both went back to the same tribe but did not hang around with each other anymore.

[Death of the boy; *Wehīx̄amōkäs*'s marriage]

So this young man lived one year. Then he died. His head came apart where *Wehīx̄amōkäs* split it open.

After his friend died, *Wehīx̄amōkäs* never went anywhere by himself and stayed with the tribe. He finally married.

[He holds up a felled tree, which pushes him into the ground]

He had a sister-in-law living. She went off down to the creek and started to chop down a tree.

At the time it was ready to fall, *Wehīx̄amōkäs* walked up just where it was going to fall. So this woman saw him just as he got even with the tree. She said, "*Wehīx̄amōkäs,* you are so powerful and can do anything; let's see you catch this tree as it falls."

He said, "Oh yes, I can catch it," and he threw his hands up. So she chopped the tree so it fell right on him.

He held the tree up, but he sank into the earth clear up to his knees—but kept the tree from the ground.

He kept on sinking till he sank into the ground till he sank to his neck, so the last word he told his sister-in-law [was:] "So! I guess I will have to leave you all. I will be back when the big general war on this earth comes off."

He spoke that whenever a little girl had a baby with the little finger cut off at the joint, that boy would be him and there would be a general war.

When he finished talking he sank into the ground. But he was still alive. It was as if someone were going someplace.[18]

98

Story of Delawares and White People

Long ago when the white man first came to this America, there was a river back east, Big River (the white name is unknown). The tribe was living there at that time, had planted their crops. They knew the whites were east of them. They elected twenty warriors. The chief instructed them to go find where the white people were, how far east they were. "You go and see where [they're] at. Do not molest them. All we want to know is how far they are from here."

So they traveled a good many days. Finally they got to a big river. They looked across it and saw lights. They said to each other, "That's where the white people are now."

So they decided to return in the morning. The twenty braves had three young men with them. That night the three young men walked off a piece and talked: "It looks very queer that those braves are simply to return and say they saw the white people, not bring any skalps [*sic*] or nothing."

But two were foolish fellows. The third was a brave but it wasn't known. So the third told the twenty what the two had said. The old men got riled. "Yes, it's all true enough," they said.

So they built a big fire, ready for war. They had a way of dancing around the fire. Each sang a song, saying he will fight now till he dies. So then the two other young *ila* had encouraged the war.

Next morning at daybreak the warriors said, "We'll go over and fight with the Big Knives. The young fellows escaped, ran off. There was one with the twenty. They started in the morning to kill all the Big Knives (*max̄aicī́ᵉkan*). They lit into war with them.

Then one young fellow was a warrior himself, went with them but did not join in the war. So the twenty fought from sunrise to sundown and all twenty were killed. About sundown the young man went back to the tribe, on his arrival saw the two young men who had been with him. So he told them, "All our warriors are all killed off by these two young men's talk. They encourage the old men to fight the people."

They all counseled together. The tribe decided to battle with the Big Knives for losing their men. So the whole tribe started toward the Big Knives' home.

So then, when they got there, war began between the Big Knives and the Delawares. So they fought for a good many days, because they were a powerful tribe of white people and a powerful tribe of Delawares.

So a good many braves among the whites were found to be as hard to kill as there were among the Delawares. So one day one of the brave men of the white people had a feeling the Delawares were going to whip [wipe?] them out, so he sent for another white brave who was on the waters, told him to come at once. They needed him.

So this man sent word he could not fight on dry land but could fight on the waters. So he sent word again that if he did not come he would loose [*sic*] his neck. So he finally came. And the Delaware for several days could not kill any of the Big Knives, though they shot at them. The bullets would not hit them.

So they got to talking and notified all the warriors to look why they could not hit any of the white warriors. There was something wrong. So they all began to look up in the clouds who were able. They saw a big fish lying between themselves and the Big Knives. Then they discovered every time they shot, they'd hit that fish. The bullets would glance up. It was a powerful fish. So they discovered right away that the white brave from the water was gifted by the fish so he could [be] protected in danger.

So at night the war stopped. They counseled. They knew it was the brave from the water that was the trouble. "That big fish is his friend."

There was a Shawnee with the Delaware. Shawnees always are with Delawares. He said, "I have a medicine that will get him"—the navy man. The fish was too powerful, but when the navy man was gone, his power would go.

At the late part of the night this medicine was completed. They made a little bow and arrow. They made a stick representing a club.[19] That white warrior went to sleep. These Indians with the medicine in front of them were in a ring. So while they were singing, when that warrior went to sleep, they were singing for that warrior to come.

A little man came to that medicine. It was that warrior's spirit. They all said, "Now, there he is."

One of the men picked up the little bow and arrow and he dipped the spearhead of the arrow in the medicine and he shot that little man. He shot him to kill him. When he shot at him the arrow bounced back as it did with the fish before.

So another said, "Pick up that club (the one the size of a match)." So they picked that club up and dipped it in that medicine. They held the club over the little man's head and dropped it. That stick killed him. So they said, "Tomorrow at noon there [will] be a big limb of a tree fall on him (that Big Knife navy man)."

So it happened the war stopped before noon. So this warrior from the waters sat in the shade of a big tree and the limb dropped off from above and broke his neck, killed him.

After they knew the time that fellow was dead, the Delawares began to whoop and went after the Big Knives again.

Where this war was, was in a deep canyon, rough rocks, and cedar stumps. So then they had a general war. There was a powerful tribe of whites and a powerful band of Delawares. They killed so many that the blood on both sides in the ditches ran like water.

So there were some women who were brave on both sides. So they counseled together and said that it was too bad they were fighting one another the way they were. The white women called the white people their children, so the Indian women called the Indian men their children. "So we'll just stop this war between our children."

So each one of those women went around notify[ing] these children to quit fighting. The war then stopped.

So the white man camped on the east side, and the Delawares on the west. So the brave from the Big Knife gang and the Indian Delaware brave met halfway between the camps. And they shook hands and said, "Well, we'll quit fighting now. We will be in peace hereafter, friends."

The Delaware said, "Tomorrow at noon I want you to come with your men and eat dinner with me, and I will show you how I eat, what I have to live on."

He went back home to the camp, and he told his young men to go out on a hunt. The hunters brought in several bears. So, early in the morning they began barbecuing this bear meat. It was stuck up on sharp sticks. This meat was strung out north and south for a long time.

The chief threw knives along there to eat with. Then he sent for the head warrior among those Big Knives. So the Big Knife warrior brought his men with him, and those old women that stopped the war brought some bread there. So they all sat down and went to eating.

After they ate dinner the Delaware warrior asked the white headman warrior, "What shall we do? We have been fighting a good many days. We've lost lots of our young men here on both sides without any cause."

The Delawares asked the white warrior, "How can we fix our treaty? Because there is a big pile of bones here on the prairie, and whenever you whites will see them, you will think of this war. And when any of my tribe comes and sees the bones, they will remember this war."

So the white warrior told the Delaware warrior, "I know what we can do so these bones will never be seen. We'll dig a big hole in the ground. We will gather up all the bodies, throw them right in that deep hole cover them up."

So the Indian warrior said, "Look here, you white people is very great to be always digging around for something. Don't you think in future times they will dig in here and find these bones and will be bound to know there was a war here?"

The white man told the Indian that it was so. The Indian was trying to figure out a treaty, so if the bones were seen it would not hurt feelings, as it was all contracted in peace: "I know of a scheme we can do. We will make a treaty that as long as the sun shows and as long as the water runs and as long as the grass grows we are to be friends and never have any war again, friends the same as brothers."

The white warrior said to the Indian, "That is certainly an everlasting binding treaty. So now I will shake hands with you for the reason there is but one god who created me and you."

So they were clasping hands. "I will never molest you or harm you any way shape or form as long as the sun shines, as the rivers flow and the grass grows. And so I further agree that I will protect you every way I can so you will not be molested by anyone (clasping his hands in front of him with fingers fitting in fingers). If anyone hits you, he will hit me first."

At the time when the Delawares and the whites made that treaty, the Delaware to this day has never violated the treaty. He does everything his brother white man tells him. So now the Delawares have come to be civilized at this day, and now they're the same as the white people.

100

Otter Skin Dance

A child had a pet otter. When the otter grew, the old folks decided to turn him loose, let him go back to where his home was or wherever he wanted.

The old man took the otter and took him far from their home. He cut off a piece of tobacco and tied it round the otter's neck in a little bag. So he talked to this otter, "Well, I am going to turn you loose. You will be at your own liberty hereafter."

So the little child didn't like it, because his pet had been freed. The old folks had turned it loose on their own account. The child wouldn't oppose it. It was simply against the child's will.

So in a short time the child took sick. They had men who were powerful and could tell the cause of things. So they doctored this sick child. So they found it was the otter that was the cause of the child being sick. So these men with power, gifted men, told this child's parents they must get an otter and get the hide and skin it whole. Then they cut the otter hide on the back, splitting it. Then these men with the power told the folks, "Likewise kill a bear and cook the bear meat."

Long in the evening they cleaned up the ground in [a] circle. They cleaned it off good. So there were two men to do the work. And they built a fire in the center where it was cleaned.

They set a fork at the east end of the fire and one at the west end. They put a pole whose bark had been peeled off across the forks. The east fork was about four [or] five steps from the limit of cleared ground. There were many forks in it. It was peeled off. The branches were sharpened. The bear was to be hung there overnight.

So all the principal old men and women were all together there that night. During the night when they first begin, the man supposed to be the relation of the sick child gets up, tells why they are there and what their intention[s] are, et cetera. He tells them that "We have found out by following these instructions given to us by the people that doctored on the child, that we were told our child would get well by following those instructions that were given to us by those men that doctored on the little child."

So then the father of this child, when they started in, got up and started the performance they had planned out. He put on the otter hide. The head was stuffed and hung down over his breast, and the tail hung down his back. He told them that he was going to take a hand in the doings.

[The text continues with a description of ceremonial procedure.]

101

When Munsees Went from Place to Place

[They were] from New York [*wuñdjiyałkuŋg*]. While they stayed there, [the] Mohawk [was their] friend. They stayed together.

Then from there they went to stay in Pennsylvania. Then [their] preacher stayed with them. Then white men crowded them out.

Then from there they went [to] Gnadenhütten. Delawares [*unāmīwak'*], too. Then Christians [came]. They lived there. They had some fields and cattle, hogs. They lived pretty good.

And then the war came. They left their land, they fled. They went west then [with] their preacher. And a long time they stayed, because there was war.

Then the white men called them to come back again to their land. The whites [said], "Come. Come back. Make friends."

Then those Munsees, they did come back again to their land. [ ] When they got there, friends told them go into the church house. "Stay there. Then we'll come there, we'll fix up friendship."

Then Munsees went thère, to the church house. There were almost a hundred of them. They waited for the whites. Then they prayed, then sang.

Then one woman's child cried. Then outdoors she took it. Then she looked up the road. Then she saw whites riding. They had big knives [*maŋgatancīKanał*].

Then she hid there in the brush. Then she looked at the whites. [They] surrounded the church house, then they entered. They began killing Indians. Blood began to pour out.

Outdoors then they burned them. There [at] the church they killed ninety-six.

Then the woman who saw what the whites did went to look for the ones who had come with them [but] hadn't gone to the church. They were hunting, they had not gone with them.

Then that woman went to look for them. Three days she walked. Then she found them, the Indians [*lenāpēwał*].

Then they went back, what few were left, [back] again to where they had fled.

Then their preacher went to Canada. Then for quite a while they stayed there.

Then they came to what is now named Kansas. There they built houses with Delawares [*delawärsał*]. Delawares [*delawärs*], their land [was] close to Kansas City.

Then the Munsees stayed there about fourteen years. Then the Delawares [*delawärsak'*] sold the land. Where Munsees lived was bought by Wyandots.

Then the Munsees went on to Leavenworth. Then they lived there seven years.

Then they moved again. They went to live with Chippewas. Now to this day, here they stayed. They stayed, became citizens.

NOTES

Introduction

1. Brinton, pp. 23, 109–13; Weslager, *History,* p. 181; Goddard, "Delaware," p. 222–23. Some students, however, interpret the designation "women" as honorific, meant to indicate that the Lenape were peacemakers (see Miller, "The Delaware as Women").

2. Bolton, pp. 126–29; cf. texts 17, 22, 28, 40, 83, 203, and 215, this volume.

3. Weslager, *History.*

4. Text 8.

5. Goddard, "Ethnohistorical Implications"; Goddard, "Delaware."

6. Weslager, *History;* Goddard, "Delaware."

7. Numbered texts may be traced in the Guide, Part Two; also in Part One.

8. Cf. Bierhorst, *Mythology of North America.*

9. Goddard, "Delaware"; Dean, "Delaware Indian Reminiscences."

10. Goddard, "Ethnohistorical Implications."

11. From here on, the word "text" is omitted in parenthetical references to texts with assigned numbers; these are traceable in the Guide, Part Two, and elsewhere in this work.

12. Text 11; cf. Zeisberger, *Dictionary,* p. 90: *Tschemámus:* "hare."

13. Texts 44, 45; cf. Zeisberger, *Dictionary,* p. 90: Mõskímus: "hare"; Delaware Nation Council, *Lunaapeew Dictionary: mooshkiingwus:* "rabbit."

14. Text 49; cf. Speck, in War Eagle, Letters, p. 111.

15. Zeisberger, *History,* p. 64; cf. text 43.

16. Harrington, *Religion,* p. 28.

17. Ibid., p. 27.

18. Ibid., p. 29; cf. Speck, "Cruising," p. 32.

19. Morgan, *Indian Journals,* p. 55; cf. Gipson, pp. 210–11.

20. Zeisberger, *History,* p. 148.

21. Harrington, Papers, Box OC-163, folder 9, no. 16.

22. Dean, "Delaware Indian Reminiscences," pp. 12–13.

23. Chafe, p. 59.

24. Curtin and Hewitt, "Seneca Fiction," pp. 799–800 and passim.

25. Goddard, "Delaware," p. 233.

26. Leland, *Algonquian Legends,* pp. 233–54.

27. Barnouw, pp. 120–31.

28. Curtin and Hewitt, "Seneca Fiction," pp. 63–64 and passim.

29. Text 2.

30. Speck, Field Notes, Grand River.

31. Speck, *Celestial Bear,* pp. 90–91.

32. The case against the Walam Olum is both linguistic and folkloristic: on the linguistic side, modern investigation has determined that all usages in the manuscript, dated 1833, are traceable to Zeisberger and Heckewelder; folkloristically, the content relates suspiciously to several sources available at the time, including Heckewelder's *History,* John Tanner's *Narrative,* and the writings of Hendrick Aupaumut (Ives Goddard and David Oestreicher, personal communications). For the linguistic evidence see Oestreicher. For an abstract of the Walam Olum see the Guide, Part Three.

33. Harrington, *Dickon,* pp. 302–3.

34. Dean, Stories in Lenape and English, side A. 2DE 18.

35. Trowbridge ms. in Weslager, *History,* p. 498. For Wehixamukes as the great hunter see text 23.

36. "Answers to the questions," in Weslager, *Westward,* p. 112; cf. ibid., p. 117, item 8.

37. Dean, Stories in Lenape and English, side A. 2DE 18.

38. Cooley, tape 686, side A.

39. Versions of Curtin's Munsee stories, reworked by J. N. B. Hewitt, had already appeared in Curtin and Hewitt's "Seneca Fiction" of 1918.

40. Harrington, *Religion,* pp. 16, 30; Harrington, "Lenape or Delaware Indians," p. 391.

Texts

1. Text 77, fully reproduced in the Guide, Part Two, is not repeated here. Text 81, preserved only in Harrington's paraphrase, has been omitted, as have texts 69, 71, 72, 76, 82, and 83, which can be read in Bierhorst, *The White Deer.* Text 68, freely adapted in Harrington's *Dickon,* does not appear to survive in manuscript.

2. Michelson's text 99, published in Bierhorst, *The White Deer,* is here omitted.

3. The translations are Michelson's lexical glosses, reordered (but not reworded), with connectives added where necessary.

4. Gloss: He is everywhere. And a further gloss: the small people, they take care of game with Misingw and drive deer away.

5. Note added: The man was Julius [Fouts's] mother's father.

6. I.e., hoofprint. A variant (text 99) has "a little pocket of water, where some livestock had tramped."

7. Consistently spelled "couldent" throughout this text.

8. Spelled "wampun" here and throughout.

9. Gloss: the scales cause the rain.

10. I.e., prayer.

11. Gloss: i.e., had a gift from those people.

12. Informant's note with transcriber's interpolations: Those (deities) represented (by the false faces) left, but the old men and fellow followed them and entered into conversation.

13. Added note: "[Wehixamukes is the] Delaware Sampson[,] says [Silas] Longbone (-k'am- release of glottis)."

14. Gloss: Wehixamokas.

15. The variant above (text 79) has "big stem of grass."

16. The odd expression "By crabs!" is repeated immediately below. Cf. "By golly!" farther below.

17. Gloss: exclamation of surprise.

18. Added notes{:} By Silas: "When W saw old people walking slowly with bent back, he would say, 'I'm going to put you out of your misery' and take out his ax. Then the person would hobble fast and try to get away. 'Gee,' said W, 'you can go pretty fast when you want to.' "

By Elkhair: "W was kind of a doctor too. He'd heal people when they were sick. But he had to be told plainly. If you said, 'Father, take pity on my child,' he would take his ax and put it out of misery. But if you said, 'Take pity and *cure* him,' he would do it."

By Silas: Similarly with lazy or sleeping persons: they would be put out of "misery."

19. Superscript gloss: As long as [a] match.

Bibliography

The asterisk (*) marks Delaware story sources, here listed with numerals in square brackets, which refer to the abstracts in the Guide, Part Two. Thus, for example, Richard C. Adams's *Legends of the Delaware Indians and Picture Writing* contains fifteen stories (abstract numbers 49–63).

Aarne, Antti, and Stith Thompson. *The Types of the Folktale.* 2d revision. Helsinki: Suomalainen Tiedeakatemia, 1973.

*Adams, Richard C. *The Ancient Religion of the Delaware Indians.* N.p., 1904. [48]

*———. *A Delaware Indian Legend and the Story of Their Troubles.* Washington, D.C., 1899. [47]

*———. *Legends of the Delaware Indians and Picture Writing.* Washington, D.C., 1905. [49–63]

*Adams, Robert H. *Songs of Our Grandfathers: Music of the Unami Delaware Indians.* Dewey, Okla.: Touching Leaves Indian Crafts, 1991. [189, 190]

*Aikens, Hannah. Family, plants, Delaware names, stories. Interview by Nicholas Shoumatoff. Cassette tape, 1977. Call no. 42 (cat. no. 2DE-8). Delaware Resource Center, Trailside Museum, Cross River, N.Y. *Note:* This and the tape described in the following entry are almost unintelligible; a partial transcript has been prepared by James Rementer and is included in his Letters on Delaware Folklore, 31 October 1990 (see Rementer, below). [186]

*———. Snake story, uses of plants. Interview by Nicholas Shoumatoff. Cassette tape, 1977. Call no. 46 (cat. no. 2DE-12). Delaware Resource Center, Trailside Museum, Cross River, N.Y. *Note:* See preceding entry for transcript by Rementer. [187, 188]

*"Answers to the questions proposed in the Pamphlet. By the Delawares and Monsies." In *The Delaware Indian Westward Migration,* C. A. Weslager, pp. 89–155. Wallingford, Pa.: Middle Atlantic Press, 1978. [26, 27]

Barbeau, Charles Marius. *Huron and Wyandot Mythology.* Canada, Department of Mines, Geological Survey, Memoir 80, Anthropological Series no. 11. Ottawa, 1915.

Barnouw, Victor. *Wisconsin Chippewa Myths and Tales.* Madison: University of Wisconsin Press, 1977.

Beauchamp, William M. *Iroquois Folk Lore.* 1922. Reprint, Port Washington, N.Y.: Kennikat Press, 1965.

Benson, Elizabeth P. "The Chthonic Canine." *Latin American Indian Literatures Journal* 7 (1991): 96–120.

Bierhorst, John. *The Mythology of Mexico and Central America.* New York: Morrow, 1990.

———. *The Mythology of North America.* New York: Morrow, 1985.

———. "Tales of the Delaware Trickster." In *Coming to Light: Contemporary Translations of the Native Literatures of North America,* ed. Brian Swann. New York: Random House, 1995.

———. *The White Deer and Other Stories Told by the Lenape.* New York: Morrow, 1995.

Boas, Franz. *Chinook Texts.* Bureau of American Ethnology, Bulletin 20, 1894.

Bolton, Reginald Pelham. *Indian Life of Long Ago in the City of New York.* 1934. Enlarged edition, New York: Harmony, 1972.

Boyd, Julian P., ed. *Indian Treaties Printed by Benjamin Franklin, 1736–1762.* Philadelphia: Historical Society of Pennsylvania, 1938.

*Brawer, Catherine Coleman. *Many Trails: Indians of the Lower Hudson Valley.* Katonah, N.Y.: Katonah Gallery, 1983. [197]

*Brinton, Daniel. *The Lenâpé and Their Legends.* 1884. Reprint, New York: AMS Press. Here included as a secondary source for Bishop John Ettwein and for an unidentified Heckewelder MS. [15, 19]

*Cass-Trowbridge MS. In *The Delaware Indian Westward Migration,* C. A. Weslager, pp. 165–205. Wallingford, Pa.: Middle Atlantic Press, 1978. [28–30]

Chafe, Wallace. *Handbook of the Seneca Language.* Albany: New York State Museum, 1963.

Converse, Harriet Maxwell. *Myths and Legends of the New York State Iroquois.* New York State Museum, Bulletin 125, 1908.

Cooley, Ralph E. Ralph E. Cooley Collection. 152 cassettes and 3 reels, numbered 545–699, dated 1977–79. Western History collection, University of Oklahoma Library, Norman, Oklahoma.

Cornplanter, Jesse J. *Legends of the Longhouse.* 1938. Reprint, Port Washington, N.Y.: Ira J. Friedman, 1963.

*Curtin, Jeremiah. MS 2204: The Legend of Moskim. National Anthropological Archives, Smithsonian Institution. [44]

*———. *Seneca Indian Myths.* New York: E. P. Dutton, 1923. *Note:* Two of the myths are Delaware. [42, 43]

*Curtin, Jeremiah, and J. N. B. Hewitt. MSS 3860, 5 boxes: Seneca Myths. National Anthropological Archives, Smithsonian Institution. *Note:* At least two of the myths are Delaware. [41, 43]

*———. "Seneca Fiction." *32nd Annual Report of the Bureau of American Ethnol-*

ogy, 1910–1911, pp. 37–819. 1918. *Note:* Comparison with Curtin, *Seneca Indian Myths,* indicates that two of the stories, nos. 28 and 110, are Delaware, though they are not here identified as such. [42, 43]

*Danckaerts, Jasper. *Journal of Jasper Danckaerts, 1679–1680.* Ed. B. B. James and J. F. Jameson. New York: Scribner's, 1913. [2]

*Dean, Nora Thompson. Delaware beliefs. Interview by Nicholas Shoumatoff. Cassette tape, 17 November 1977. Call no. 53b (cat. no. 2DE-19). Delaware Resource Center, Trailside Museum, Cross River, N.Y. [183–85]

*———. "Delaware Indian Reminiscences." Interview by Andrew Twaddle, January 1975. *Bulletin of the Archaeological Society of New Jersey* 35 (1978): 1–17. [164–71]

———. *Lenape Language Lessons.* Lessons One and Two. 2d ed. Dewey, Oklahoma: Touching Leaves Indian Crafts, 1989.

*———. Place names, visions, stories. Interview by Nicholas Shoumatoff. Cassette tape, 1976. Call no. 16 (cat. no. C-2 and/or L-15). Delaware Resource Center, Trailside Museum, Cross River, N.Y. [174, 175]

*———. Stories in Lenape and English. Interview by Nicholas Shoumatoff. Cassette tape, 17 November 1977. Call no. 52a (cat. no. 2DE-18 and/or 2DE-21). Delaware Resource Center, Trailside Museum, Cross River, N.Y. [176–82]

Delaware Nation Council. *Lunaapeew Dictionary: Basic Words.* Part 1. Thamesville, Ontario: Delaware Nation Council, Moravian of the Thames Band, 1992.

Dorsey, George A. *The Pawnee: Mythology.* Washington, D.C.: Carnegie Institution of Washington, 1906.

———. *Traditions of the Arikara.* Washington, D.C.: Carnegie Institution of Washington, 1904.

———. *Traditions of the Caddo.* Washington, D.C.: Carnegie Institution of Washington, 1905.

*Ellis, Martha. The Mother-in-Law Story. 1979. Typescript, copy in the possession of James Rementer. *Note:* A copy is included in Rementer, Letters on Delaware Folklore, 4 September 1990 (see Rementer, below). [214]

Fenton, William N. *The False Faces of the Iroquois.* Norman: University of Oklahoma Press, 1987.

———. Review of *The Celestial Bear Comes Down to Earth,* by Frank G. Speck. *American Anthropologist* 48 (1946): 423–27.

Fisher, Margaret W. "The Mythology of the Northern and Northeastern Algonkians in Reference to Algonkian Mythology as a Whole." In *Man in Northeastern North America,* ed. Frederick Johnson, pp. 226–62. Andover, Mass.: Phillips Academy, 1946.

Genovese, Eugene D. *Roll, Jordan, Roll: The World the Slaves Made.* New York: Random House, 1976.

*Gilliland, Lula Mae Gibson. MS 3873, notebook 3: This is the True Religion of the Delaware Indian Tribe. 1947. National Anthropological Archives, Smithsonian Institution. [136–38]

*Gipson, Lawrence Henry. *The Moravian Indian Mission on the White River: Diaries and Letters, May 5, 1799, to November 12, 1806*. Indianapolis: Indiana Historical Bureau, 1938. [20]

Goddard, Ives. "Delaware." In *Handbook of North American Indians,* ed. William C. Sturtevant. Vol. 15, *Northeast,* pp. 213–39. Washington, D.C.: Smithsonian Institution, 1978.

———. *Delaware Verbal Morphology*. New York: Garland, 1979.

———. "The Ethnohistorical Implications of Early Delaware Linguistic Materials." *Man in the Northeast* 1 (1971): 14–26.

Goodsky, Harold. Interview in *The Sacred: Ways of Knowledge, Sources of Life,* Peggy V. Beck and Anna L. Walters, pp. iv, 206–7. Tsaile, Arizona: Navajo Community College Press, 1977.

*Gowing, Clara. Indian Traditions. MS 4p. Kansas State Historical Society, Topeka. [37–39]

Grinnell, George Bird. *Blackfeet Indian Stories*. New York: Scribner's, 1913.

———. *Pawnee Hero Stories and Folk-Tales*. 1889. Reprint, Lincoln: University of Nebraska Press, 1961.

Hadlock, Wendell S. "The Concept of Tribal Separation as Rationalized in Indian Folklore." *Pennsylvania Archaeologist* 16 (1946): 84–90.

*Hale, Duane K., ed. *Cooley's Traditional Stories of the Delaware*. Anadarko, Okla.: Delaware Tribe of Western Oklahoma Press, 1984. [191–94]

*———. *Turtle Tales: Oral Traditions of the Delaware Tribe of Western Oklahoma*. Anadarko, Okla.: Delaware Tribe of Western Oklahoma Press, 1984. [198–210]

*Harrington, M. R. *The Indians of New Jersey: Dickon Among the Lenapes*. New Brunswick, N.J.: Rutgers University Press, 1963. (Originally published as *Dickon Among the Lenape Indians*. New York: Holt, Rinehart and Winston, 1938). [68, 69–71]

———. "Lenape or Delaware Indians." In *American Indian Life,* ed. Elsie Clews Parsons. 1922. Reprint, Lincoln: University of Nebraska Press, 1967.

*———. Papers. Museum of the American Indian, Archives. Box OC-160, folder 1; Box OC-161, folder 1; Box OC-163, folder 9. [67, 69–87]

*———. "A Preliminary Sketch of Lenápe Culture." *American Anthropologist* 15 (1913): 208–35. [65]

*———. *Religion and Ceremonies of the Lenape*. New York: Museum of the American Indian, 1921. [75, 88–92]

*———. "Some Customs of the Delaware Indians." *The Museum Journal* 1 (1910): 52–60. University of Pennsylvania. [64]

*Heckewelder, John. *History, Manners and Customs of the Indian Nations Who Once Inhabited Pennsylvania and the Neighboring States.* Ed. William C. Reichel. Philadelphia: Historical Society of Pennsylvania, 1876. [16–18]

*———. "Indian Tradition of the First Arrival of the Dutch at Manhattan Island, Now New-York." *Collections of the New York Historical Society,* 2d ser., vol. 1, pp. 69–74. New York, 1841. Essentially the same as Heckewelder's *History,* ch. 2. [17]

*———. *A Narrative of the Mission of the United Brethren Among the Delaware and Mohegan Indians.* Philadelphia: M'Carty and Davis, 1820. [7]

*Hewitt, J. N. B. MS 16, Cosmologic Legend. National Anthropological Archives, Smithsonian Institution. [45]

*———. "Iroquoian Cosmology," first part. *21st Annual Report of the Bureau of American Ethnology, 1899–1900,* pp. 127–339. 1903. *Note:* One version of the Iroquoian creation myth is from the Delaware speaker John Armstrong. [46]

———. "Iroquoian Cosmology," second part. *43d Annual Report of the Bureau of American Ethnology, 1925–1926,* pp. 449–819. 1928.

*Howard, James H. *Shawnee!* Athens, Ohio: Ohio University Press, 1981. [197]

Hultkranz, Ake. *The North American Indian Orpheus Tradition.* Statens Etnografiska Museum Monograph Series 2. Stockholm, 1957.

Hunter, Charles E. "The Delaware Nativist Revival of the Mid-Eighteenth Century." *Ethnohistory* 13 (1971): 39–49.

Jacobs, Elizabeth Derr. *Nehalem Tillamook Tales.* Eugene: University of Oregon Books, 1959.

*Jefferson, Thomas. *Notes on the State of Virginia.* Ed. William Peden. Chapel Hill: University of North Carolina Press, 1955. [8]

Jenness, Diamond. *The Ojibwa Indians of Parry Island: Their Social and Religious Life.* National Museum of Canada, Bulletin 78. Anthropological Series 17. Ottawa, 1935.

Jones, James Athearn. *Traditions of the North American Indians: Being a Second and Revised Edition of "Tales of an Indian Camp [pub. 1829]."* 3 vols. London: Colburn and Bentley, 1830.

Jones, Peter. *History of the Ojebway Indians.* 1861. Reprint, Freeport, N.Y.: Books for Libraries Press, 1970.

———. *Life and Journals of Kah-ke-wa-quo-nā-by.* Toronto: A. Green, 1860.

Kalm, Peter. *Peter Kalm's Travels in North America.* Ed. Adolph B. Benson. 2 vols. New York: Dover, 1966.

Kilpatrick, Jack F., and Anna G. Kilpatrick. *Friends of Thunder: Folktales of the Oklahoma Cherokees.* Dallas: Southern Methodist University Press, 1964.

Kinietz, Vernon. *Delaware Culture Chronology.* Indianapolis: Indiana Historical Society, 1946.

———, ed. *Meearmeear Traditions: C. C. Trowbridge's Account.* Occasional Papers of the Museum of Anthropology, no. 7. Ann Arbor: University of Michigan, 1938.

Kinietz, Vernon, and E. W. Voegelin, eds. *Shawnese Traditions: C. C. Trowbridge's Account.* Occasional Papers of the Museum of Anthropology, no. 9. Ann Arbor: University of Michigan, 1939.

*Kraft, Herbert C. *The Lenape: Archaeology, History, and Ethnography.* Newark: New Jersey Historical Society, 1986. [152]

*Kraft, Herbert C., and John T. Kraft. *The Lenape Indians of Lenapehoking.* South Orange, N.J.: Seton Hall University Museum, 1985. [153]

Leach, Douglas Edward. "Colonial Indian Wars." In *Handbook of North American Indians,* ed. William C. Sturtevant. Vol. 4, *History of Indian-White Relations,* pp. 128–43. Washington, D.C.: Smithsonian Institution, 1988.

Leach, Maria, and Jerome Fried, eds. *Standard Dictionary of Folklore, Mythology, and Legend.* New York: Funk and Wagnalls, 1972.

Leland, Charles Godfrey. *The Algonquin Legends of New England.* Boston: Houghton, Mifflin, 1884.

*Leland, Charles Godfrey, and John Dyneley Prince. *Kulóskap the Master and Other Algonkin Poems.* New York: Funk and Wagnalls, 1902. [66]

*Lindeström, Peter. *Geographia Americae.* Trans. Amandus Johnson. Philadelphia: Swedish Colonial Society, 1925. [1]

*Loskiel, George Henry. *History of the Mission of the United Brethren Among the Indians in North America.* Trans. C. I. LaTrobe. London: The Brethren Society for the Furtherance of the Gospel, 1794. *Note:* Material evidently derived from Zeisberger and later published in Zeisberger's *History* has been assigned to that title, q.v. [14]

Mallery, Garrick. *Picture Writing of the American Indians.* 2 vols. 1893. Reprint, New York: Dover, 1972.

Marriott, Alice, and Carol K. Rachlin. *American Indian Mythology.* New York: New American Library, 1972.

Mechling, W. H. *Malecite Tales.* Canada, Department of Mines, Geological Survey, Memoir 49, Anthropological Series no. 4. Ottawa, 1914.

*Michelson, Truman. MS 2776. Ethnological and Linguistic Field Notes from the Munsee in Kansas and the Delaware in Oklahoma. National Anthropological Archives, Smithsonian Institution. [93–101]

Miller, Jay. "The Delaware as Women: A Symbolic Solution." *American Ethnologist* 1 (1974): 507–14.

*Montour, Josiah. Texts. 1931. Item 1173. Manuscripts Relating to the American Indian. American Philosophical Society, Philadelphia. [105–7]

*Morgan, Lewis Henry. *The Indian Journals, 1859–62*. Ed. Leslie A. White. Ann Arbor: University of Michigan Press, 1959. [33–36]

*Moses, Jesse. Del[aware,] Jesse Moses, Story of Indian Summer. One page written in Speck's (?) hand, included among Letters to Frank G. Speck, 1934–38. Item 893. Manuscripts Relating to the American Indian. American Philosophical Society, Philadelphia. [124]

Myrtle, Minnie. *The Iroquois*. New York: Appleton, 1855.

*Newcomb, William W., Jr. *The Culture and Acculturation of the Delaware Indians*. Anthropological Papers, no. 10. Ann Arbor: University of Michigan, Museum of Anthropology, 1956. [139–48]

Oestreicher, David M. "Unmasking the *Walam Olum*: A 19th-Century Hoax." *Bulletin of the Archaeological Society of New Jersey* 49 (1994): 1–44.

Parker, Arthur C. *Seneca Myths and Folk Tales*. 1923. Reprint, New York: AMS Press, 1978.

*Parker, William B. "Manners, Customs, and History of the Indians of South-Western Texas." In *Information Respecting the History, Condition and Prospects of the Indian Tribes . . .*, ed. H. R. Schoolcraft. Vol. 5, pp. 682–85. Philadelphia: Lippincott, 1856. [32]

*Pearson, Bruce L. *A Grammar of Delaware*. Dewey, Okla.: Touching Leaves Indian Crafts, 1988. (Ph.D. diss., University of California, Berkeley, 1972.) [151]

*———. Notebook, August 1969. Contains stories in Delaware told by Nora Thompson Dean, transcribed from an audio tape with interlinear English glosses. In the possession of B. Pearson, Department of English, University of South Carolina, Columbia. [155, 156, 157–60]

*Petrullo, Vincenzo. *The Diabolic Root: A Study of Peyotism, the New Indian Religion, Among the Delawares*. Philadelphia: University of Pennsylvania Press, 1934. [109–12]

*Prince, J. Dyneley. "A Modern Delaware Tale." *Proceedings of the American Philosophical Society* 41 (1902): 20–34. [66]

———. *Passamaquoddy Texts*. Publications of the American Ethnological Society. Vol. 10, 1921.

Pullum, Geoffrey K., and William A. Ladusaw. *Phonetic Symbol Guide*. Chicago: University of Chicago Press, 1986.

Rafinesque, C. S. Walamolum. 1833. MS. Special Collections, Van Pelt Library, University of Pennsylvania, Philadelphia. *Note:* A photographic facsimile of the MS is in the library of the University Museum, University of Pennsylvania.

Rand, Silas T. *Legends of the Micmacs*. New York and London: Longmans, Green, 1894.

Redfield, Robert. Notes on San Antonio Palopo. Microfilm Collection of Manuscripts on Cultural Anthropology, no. 4. 1945. Joseph Regenstein Library, University of Chicago.

*Rementer, James A. "Delaware Indian Humor." *Bulletin of the Archaeological Society of New Jersey* 47 (1992): 69–75.

*———. Letters on Delaware Folklore and Other Delaware Topics, 1990–93. Manuscripts Relating to the American Indian. American Philosophical Society, Philadelphia. [161–63, 211–13, 215–18]

*Rementer, James. A., ed. Christmas letters based on texts by Nora Thompson Dean, sent to friends and customers of Touching Leaves Indian Crafts, Dewey, Okla., 1968–92. Manuscripts Relating to the American Indian. American Philosophical Society, Philadelphia. [149–54, 162, 178, 196]

Rose, H. J. *A Handbook of Greek Mythology, Including Its Extension to Rome.* New York: Dutton, 1959.

Rudes, Blair A., and Dorothy Crouse, eds. *The Tuscarora Legacy of J. N. B. Hewitt: Materials for the Study of Tuscarora Language and Culture.* Canadian Ethnology Service, paper no. 108. National Museums of Canada, 1987.

Schorer, C. E. "Indian Tales of C. C. Trowbridge: The Man Eater Spirit." *Southern Folklore Quarterly* 29 (1965): 309–18.

Schutz, Noel W[illiam]. "The Study of Shawnee Myth in an Ethnographic and Ethnohistorical Perspective." Ph.D. diss., Indiana University, 1975. Copy at IU Libraries, Bloomington. *Note:* This work includes unpublished myths collected by Schutz and by C. F. Voegelin.

Silverberg, Robert. *Mammoths, Mastodons and Man.* New York: McGraw-Hill, 1970.

Skinner, Alanson. "Notes on Mahikan Ethnology." *Bulletin of the Public Museum of the City of Milwaukee* 2, no. 3 (1925): 87–116. (The migration legend on pp. 101–2 is apparently derived from or related to the narrative of Hendrick Aupaumut; see Brinton, *Lenâpé and Their Legends,* p. 20, and Sturtevant, *Handbook of North American Indians,* vol. 15, p. 809).

———. "Some Aspects of the Folk-Lore of the Central Algonkin." *Journal of American Folklore* 27 (1914): 97–100.

Smith, Erminie. *Myths of the Iroquois.* 1883. Reprint, Ohsweken, Ontario: Iroqrafts, 1983.

*Snake, Bessie. Cutting the Hide Story. Typescript, n.d., copy in the possession of James Rementer. *Note:* A copy is included in Rementer, Letters on Delaware Folklore, 18 June 1991 (see Rementer, above). [215]

*Speck, Frank G. "The Boy-bear." *Anthropos* 35–36 (1940–41): 973–74. [122]

*———. *The Celestial Bear Comes Down to Earth.* Reading, Pa.: Reading Museum and Art Gallery, 1945. [118–20, 122, 123]

———. "Cruising the Eastern Woods with a Delaware Chief." *Pennsylvania Archaeologist* 16 (1946): 31–33.

———. *Ethnology of the Yuchi.* Philadelphia: University [of Pennsylvania] Museum, 1909.

———. Field Notes, Grand River, 1946. Item 181. Manuscripts Relating to the American Indian. American Philosophical Society, Philadelphia.

———. *Naskapi.* 1935. Reprint, Norman: University of Oklahoma Press, 1977.

*———. *Oklahoma Delaware Ceremonies, Feasts and Dances.* Philadelphia: American Philosophical Society, 1937. [113–17]

———. *Penobscot Man.* Philadelphia: University of Pennsylvania Press, 1940.

———. "Penobscot Tales and Religious Beliefs." *Journal of American Folklore* 48 (1935): 1–107.

*———. *A Study of the Delaware Indian Big House Ceremony.* Harrisburg: Pennsylvania Historical Commission, 1931. [102–4]

Speck, Frank G., and Wendell S. Hadlock. "A Report on Tribal Boundaries and Hunting Areas of the Malecite Indian of New Brunswick." *American Anthropologist* 48 (1946): 355–64.

Stands in Timber, John, and Margot Liberty, with Robert M. Utley. *Cheyenne Memories.* New Haven: Yale University Press, 1967.

Strachey, William. *The Historie of Travell into Virginia Britania.* London: Hakluyt Society, 1953.

Sturtevant, William C., ed. *Handbook of North American Indians.* Vol. 15, *Northeast.* Washington, D.C.: Smithsonian Institution, 1978.

Swanton, John. *Early History of the Creek Indians and Their Neighbors.* Bureau of American Ethnology, Bulletin 73. 1922.

———. "Mythology of the Indians of Louisiana and the Texas Coast." *Journal of American Folklore* 20 (1907): 285–89.

———. *Myths and Tales of the Southeastern Indians.* Bureau of American Ethnology, Bulletin 88. 1929.

Tanner, Adrian. *Bringing Home Animals: Religious Ideology and Mode of Production of the Mistassini Cree Hunters.* New York: St. Martin's, 1979.

Tanner, John. *A Narrative of the Captivity and Adventures of John Tanner During Thirty Years Residence Among the Indians in the Interior of North America.* Ed. Edwin James. Minneapolis: Ross and Haines, 1956.

*Tantaquidgeon, Gladys. *A Study of Delaware Indian Medicine Practice and Folk Beliefs.* Harrisburg: Pennsylvania Historical Commission, 1942. [131, 132, 134]

Thompson, Stith. *European Tales Among American Indians.* Colorado College Publication, Language Series, vol. 2, no. 34. Colorado Springs, Colorado, 1919.

———. *The Folktale.* New York: Holt, Rinehart and Winston, 1946.

———. *Motif-Index of Folk-Literature.* 6 vols. Bloomington: Indiana University Press, 1955.

———. *Tales of the North American Indians.* 1929. Reprint, Bloomington: Indiana University Press, 1966.

*Trowbridge MS In *The Delaware Indians: A History,* C. A. Weslager, pp. 473–500. New Brunswick, N.J.: Rutgers University Press, 1972. [21–25]

Van der Donck, Adriaen. *A Description of the New Netherlands.* Ed. Thomas F. O'Donnell. Syracuse: Syracuse University Press, 1968.

Van Laan, Nancy. *Rainbow Crow: A Lenape Tale.* New York: Knopf, 1989.

Voegelin, Carl F. "Delaware, an Eastern Algonquian Language." In *Linguistic Structures of Native America,* ed. Harry Hoijer. New York: Viking Fund, 1946.

*———. Delaware Songs and Texts. N.d. Item 4225b. Manuscripts Relating to the American Indian. American Philosophical Society, Philadelphia. [128]

*———. "Delaware Texts." *International Journal of American Linguistics* 11 (1945): 105–19. [125–27]

———. *The Shawnee Female Deity.* Yale University Publications in Anthropology, no. 10. 1936.

Wallace, Anthony F. C., and William D. Reyburn. "Crossing the Ice: A Migration Legend of the Tuscarora Indians." *International Journal of American Linguistics* 17 (1951): 42–47.

*War Eagle [better known as C. C. Webber, Charley Webber, James C. Webber, etc.]. Delaware Witchcraft. [11 December 1939.] Item 929. Manuscripts Relating to the American Indian. American Philosophical Society, Philadelphia. [129]

*———. Legend of Snow Boy. [March 1933.] Item 930. Manuscripts Relating to the American Indian. American Philosophical Society, Philadelphia. [108]

*———. Legend of Woods Dwarf. Item 931. Manuscripts Relating to the American Indian. American Philosophical Society, Philadelphia. [133]

*———. Letters to Frank G. Speck. [1929–1945.] Item 932. Manuscripts Relating to the American Indian. American Philosophical Society, Philadelphia. [121, 130, 135]

Warren, William W. *History of the Ojibway Nation.* Minneapolis: Ross and Haines, 1957. (Originally published as "History of the Ojibways, Based upon Traditions and Oral Statements," *Collections of the Minnesota Historical Society* 5 [1885]: 29–394.)

*Waubuno, Chief [called John Wampum per Harrington, *Religion and Ceremonies,* p. 21]. *The Traditions of the Delawares.* 4th ed. London: Bowers Brothers, [1875 per Rutgers University Libraries]. *Note:* Most of Waubuno's "Munsee" material is Ojibwa, copied from Peter Jones's *History* and *Life and Journals.* [40]

Waugh, F. W. Collection of Iroquois Folklore. Typescript. Canadian Ethnology

Service, National Museums of Canada. Hull, Quebec. (A carbon copy is MS 1666, American Philosophical Society, Philadelphia.)

Webber, James C. See War Eagle.

*Weslager, C. A. *The Delaware Indian Westward Migration.* Wallingford, Pa.: Middle Atlantic Press, 1978.

*———. *The Delaware Indians: A History.* New Brunswick, N.J.: Rutgers University Press, 1972.

Wheeler-Voegelin, Erminie, and Remedios W. Moore. "The Emergence Myth in Native North America." In *Studies in Folklore,* ed. W. Edson Richmond. Bloomington: Indiana University Press, 1957.

Williams, Mentor L., ed. *Schoolcraft's Indian Legends.* East Lansing: Michigan State University Press, 1956.

Williams, Roger. *A Key into the Language of America.* London: Gregory Dexter, 1643.

"Willie's Tales." *Time,* 7 August 1939, p. 45.

*Witthoft, John. "The 'Grasshopper War' Folktale." *Journal of American Folklore* 66 (1953): 295–301. [31]

Witthoft, John, and Wendell S. Hadlock. "Cherokee-Iroquois Little People." *Journal of American Folklore* 59 (1946): 413–22.

*Wolley, Charles. *Two Years' Journal in New York.* 1902. Reprint, Harrison, N.Y.: Harbor Hill Books, 1973. [3–5]

*Zeisberger, David. *David Zeisberger's History of the Northern American Indians.* Ed. A. B. Hulbert and W. N. Schwarze. Ohio State Archaeological and Historical Society, 1910. [9–13]

———. *Zeisberger's Indian Dictionary.* Cambridge, Mass.: John Wilson and Son, 1887.

Index

Entries are keyed to the abstract numbers (*see* Guide, Part Two) rather than page numbers.

About the Author

John Bierhorst's books on Native American literature include *The Mythology of North America*, *The Mythology of Mexico and Central America*, and *Four Masterworks of American Indian Literature*. His articles and reviews have appeared in *Journal of American Folklore*, *Ethnohistory*, *New Scholar*, and *The New York Times Book Review*. Ranging widely in the fields of Native literature and music, his research has been supported by grants from the Americas Foundation, the Center for Inter-American Relations, the Columbia Translation Center, the National Endowment for the Arts, and the National Endowment for the Humanities. His books have been translated into Spanish, German, Polish, and Italian. A specialist in Aztec studies, he is the editor-translator of *History and Mythology of the Aztecs: The Codex Chimalpopoca*, and the author of a Nahuatl-English dictionary. He has served as a reviewer and panelist for the National Endowment for the Humanities, as an editorial advisor for the Smithsonian Series of Studies in Native American Literatures, and, most recently, as an editor of *The Norton Anthology of World Masterpieces*.

9 780816 515738